Reflections
from the
Riverfront

**Essays on Life in the Mississippi
National River and Recreation Area**

TIM SPITZACK

Reflections from the Riverfront

Published in the United States of America by:
Saint Paul Publishing Co.
1643 S. Robert Street, Suite 60B
West St. Paul, MN 55118

Cover design: Photo of the St. Paul riverfront at Harriet Island Regional Park, St. Paul, Minnesota

The essays in this book first appeared in the St. Paul Voice newspaper. Associated Press style has been maintained for this book. Some articles have been edited slightly to provide updated information.

ISBN: 978-0-9862897-0-5

FOR
Those who understand that you don't have
to travel far to find true adventure.

Contents

Observation

Contemplation

Exploration

Introduction

In November 1988, the United States Congress passed legislation to establish the Mississippi National River and Recreation Area (MNRRA), a 72-mile corridor along the river in the Twin Cities of Minneapolis-St. Paul that the National Park Service protects and enhances in partnership with a variety of city, county and state agencies. The name given to this unit of the Park Service is a mouthful but what the legislation did was monumental. It effectively created a national park in the heart of a major metropolitan area. And yet if you ask the few million who live, work or play within its boundaries where MNRRA is, you'll likely get a blank stare.

MNRRA is a unique yet widely under-recognized national park. The Park Service owns no land within its boundaries, except for a few islands within the river and 29 acres in South Minneapolis that it acquired in 2010. As a result, it works in partnership with city, county and state agencies in the Twin Cities metropolitan area to create an interconnected zone of parks, trails and green spaces. It is for this reason that most don't associate the area with the national park that it is. To them it is the city or county park where they picnic during the summer, the trail along the river where they bike or hike, the place they fish or boat.

Congress created this park because of its historical, recreational, scenic, cultural, natural, economic and scientific importance. From where the Crow River spills into the Mississippi near Dayton to the floodplain below Hastings, the river travels through wild and scenic areas, past industrial sites and along the shore of two major cities. The opportunities to experience the river are endless. I can attest to that. Since 1999, I've spent much of my recreational time in this park. It has captured my heart and continues to thrill me.

This book is about my time in the park. It is divided into three sections. The first is a collection of nature essays that celebrate the river robed in its seasonal splendor.

The second part is a series of articles I wrote on life in the river valley. I spent a half hour sitting on a bench along the river on the first Friday of each month for an entire year to contemplate and reflect upon life in a river town.

Finally, the third part is a series written about the park's many amenities. My adventures included a high-brow meal and concert at a jazz club in downtown Minneapolis, geocaching near a historic fort, riding a passenger train through the river valley and spending a romantic evening aboard one of the country's few floating bed and breakfast inns.

I love the park for all that it offers: recreation and history, contemporary culture and commerce, and the movement of everyday life. Every mile of the river offers a memory to be made. I invite you to explore some of mine, and I invite you to experience the park and the river yourself to make some of your own.

Part I

Essays on the River

Summer Snow

June 2014

In the Upper Mississippi River Valley we generally view summer as that carefree time between Memorial Day and Labor Day. These dozen or so weeks are seen as a gift and cherished as such. We eagerly await the season with thoughts of leisure and slowing our pace but when it arrives we rip into it like a kid tearing into a colorful Christmas package. It's a time of year people flock to the river to boat, hike, bike, fish, picnic or engage in a number of other outdoor endeavors. The days are gloriously long and we stuff as much activity as possible into them.

Midway through summer we finally exhale. We

have already enjoyed many of the recreational pursuits we dreamed of months earlier and enough outdoor chores have been checked off our list that guilt's claws recede and even a gentle breeze can blow that monster off our back. Eventually, the heat of mid-summer forces us to slow down, and it's then that we finally find rest. We discover it on the warm sands of a beach, in a hammock in our own backyard, or beneath the shade of a tree in a riverside park.

Nothing says summer better than resting beneath the shade of a large tree, and there is no better tree for shade than the cottonwood. They are stalwarts of the river valley that grow up to 80 feet high with a canopy that spreads out just as wide. Their distinctive trunks have massive girth, growing to four feet in diameter, and their deeply grooved bark resembles the face of an ancient wise man. They are not a popular tree for yards because their strong roots wreak havoc on sewer systems and the cotton they shed in early summer clogs window screens, but in the heat of summer they are our closest friend.

Cottonwoods thrive in floodplains and were a welcomed sight and source of refuge to trail-weary pioneers who traveled across the vast prairie in this region. They are a fast-growing tree but have declined in numbers locally over the past few decades due to riverfront development and other factors. This has prompted the Mississippi River Fund to lead an effort this summer to reforest the area with them. These trees are a critical nesting habitat for bald eagles and are instrumental in controlling riverbank erosion. According to the Minnesota Department of Natural Resources, Minnesota has one of the largest populations of nesting bald eagles in the United States. There are approximately 50 active nests in the Twin Cities area, and more than 700 breeding areas in the state, which is nearly 45 percent more than 25 years ago. Eagles love cottonwood trees because they can support their huge nests, which are commonly six to eight feet wide. An estimated 84 percent of bald eagles in the Mississippi National River and Recreation Area nest in cottonwood trees.

This iconic riverfront tree is prevalent in Harriet Island Regional Park in St. Paul so I drove there in early June to see them. I didn't make it past the east entrance gate before I started seeing summer snow. I parked my car and walked a short distance to a beautiful textbook cottonwood. It was huge. I wondered just how big so I used a rudimentary method to measure it. Putting one foot directly in front of the other and circling the tree I estimated it to be 26 feet in circumference. I looked up and marveled at how high it stretched toward the heavens. Its sturdy limbs reached out far and wide like ever-protective arms. I stepped off the width of the canopy: 85 feet.

I walked away from the tree to get a full view of it and saw that it was stuffed with cotton, hanging like Spanish moss from its waxy, heart shaped leaves. It was breezy, and each gust brought the tree to life. Its leaves seemed to sing in chorus and laugh as the tree tossed

The cool days of October are like a finger tapping us on the shoulder, reminding us to make the most of the fleeting days of fall. We fill these days with outdoor chores and recreation, and when they are over we realize how busy we have been in recent months. We put on sweaters and jackets, pull zippers to our chin and exhale. Eventually, we retreat to the safety of indoors and stoke a fire in the hearth. Conversation is shared over coffee or tea. And the dreaming begins.

Sleep Well Old Man River

December 2010

Around Thanksgiving Day each year the last towboat of the shipping season quietly slips out of St. Paul, pushing the final barges of commodities downriver. To most, it's a non-monumental event. However, to those who work in the shipping industry it's a significant yearly milestone. It's a time when river life downshifts to a much slower pace. In recent weeks, a whirlwind of activity has taken place on the river as corn, soybeans, wheat and other commodities are shipped from St. Paul to distant ports.

Now the ever-present drone of the large diesel

engines of the towboats is gone and the river is quiet, save for the outboard motors of a few hardy sportsmen who will troll the waters until they freeze over. After the barges are gone, the river, made choppy by the gales of November, appears restless, as if it feels guilty for clocking out and heading home. It's a working river, a blue-collar river, and it is accustomed to hard work. But the biting northern winds of December help settle it down. The freezing temperatures of the coming weeks will remind the river that it has completed a job well-done and that it is now OK to rest. And rest it will.

It's a slow process to quiet the mighty Mississippi. At first a thin sheet of ice will form near its banks, and with each passing day and the falling of temperature, the river will move a little slower, become a little calmer. Slowly but surely the crust of ice accumulates inward until it eventually wraps the river in a frozen blanket for a long winter's nap. During this time, the river will receive a welcome respite from the pressures we thrust upon it. No longer will diesel fuel and oil find its way into the river, nor will polluted storm water run-off from our lawns and businesses, or trash left behind by unsympathetic recreationalists.

However, even as the river rests, it is still alive, ever moving. It traps oxygen beneath its icy blanket to support the fish and other aquatic life that live below, and it never stops roaming between its shores. A few short months from now, after it is well-rested, the river will throw back its blanket and proclaim, "I'm ready to work. I'm ready to play." And we'll be glad it is.

Thoughts of a First Snow

December 2014

I welcomed December with a walk along the Mississippi River. It was an enjoyable hike and I was surprised at how much of the river was visible through the forest with the leaves now underfoot rather than overhead, but something was missing. December never looks right to me until she's wearing her wedding gown. I wished for snow and the next day my wish was granted.

It was a Monday afternoon and the sky slowly turned gray. Suddenly, the snow that was predicted for the northern part of our state dipped down to greet

Clifford Larson recounts some of that fun surrounding the first St. Paul Winter Carnival. In those days, they cut blocks of ice from the river for an ice castle and built massive toboggan and sleigh runs on the bluffs, including a half-mile toboggan slide on Ramsey Hill, a 9-block run on Dayton's Bluff and a 2,000-foot shoot on Crocus Hill that began with a steep 90-foot drop. People skated on the river, ice-fished the river, and raced sleighs on the river.

Today, people continue to turn out in droves for the Winter Carnival to run races, make art from snow and ice, and parade through cold and windy downtown streets. And to cap it off, they gather near the river at nighttime to watch as the sky is lit up like the Fourth of July. It's proof that we are still willing to embrace winter and to make the most of it, which is fortunate because March — one of the snowiest months of the year — is just around the corner.

Equal, but Rarely Ever Fair

May 2014

The arrival of the vernal equinox is a time of celebration, albeit one that is often mixed with trepidation. The Latin-derived name for the first day of spring suggests equal day and night because on March 20 we experience approximately the same amount of daylight and darkness. However, even though that day might be equal, it's rarely ever fair, as evidenced by my trip to Fort Snelling State Park the weekend following the turning of the season.

A program entitled "Desperately Seeking Spring" caught my attention so I headed to the park and joined a handful of others who were longing for the end of my chin and walk briskly to a bench near the riverfront. More than a dozen benches are scattered throughout the park, all empty, so I have my pick. I choose one that is near the middle of the park, one that affords me a good view of the river and the surrounding area.

It's not long before people begin to pass by. Some are young, some old, but all are dressed for their activity. The runners and bikers wear light, breathable attire, while the walkers are covered in sweatshirts and polar fleece; some even don heavy winter jackets and puffy ear muffs. All pass by without looking directly at me. They are engaged in conversation, the exertion of their sport, or are deep in thought. An elderly couple walks by hand-in-hand, silent. A group of women follows them and I hear a fragmented conversation about a difficult workplace situation. Nearby, a young couple stands on opposite sides of a massive cottonwood tree. I watch as they wrap themselves around it and try to clasp each other's hands. Unsuccessful, they step back, smile broadly and continue on their way.

Upriver are the boats of the Padelford Riverboat Company, which this spring mourned the passing of its founder, Captain Bill Bowell. Downstream the boys at Upper River Services are busy moving barges around the harbor so a towboat can take them downriver. Soon the last of the barges will be gone and about nine million tons of commodities will have been shipped to distant ports. I wonder if some of the crew on the last trip south will ride the season all the way to New Orleans and experience the height of autumn in ten states. In New Orleans today it is not much warmer than here — 64 degrees — but the forecast calls for upper 70s in the coming days. Ours calls for lower 40s.

This past weekend, while watching the Minnesota Vikings squeak out a victory in North Carolina and seeing the warm, sunny weather surrounding the stadium, my brother-in-law posed the question: "Why do we live in Minnesota?" It's a fair question, especially from someone who grew up on the Iron Range and endured his share of brutal winters. It's a question that occupies our conversations as we brace ourselves for the approaching season. Many are hustling to complete outdoor chores before the snow arrives, and I'm no different. This week I purchased firewood, cleaned our windows and garage, and am planning to spend the weekend mulching the countless leaves blanketing my yard.

Winter is coming, and with it the festive holiday season. Across the river I can see the St. Paul Library. It overlooks Rice Park, which becomes a winter wonderland in December and is home to St. Paul's Christmas tree, thousands of holiday lights and other seasonal decorations.

I glance at my watch and see that my time has expired. A brittle, heart-shaped cottonwood leaf is shaken from the tree overhead and gently spins its way into the cold river. It floats with others in the quiet water near the river's edge. Waiting.

December 2, 2011
12:30 p.m.
31 degrees F
Sunny; cold breeze

Harriet Island Regional Park looks much different today. It is empty and quiet and the leaves have vanished from the trees, leaving them naked, twiggy and gnarled. From the parking lot I notice the great lawn is filled with about 150 Canada geese. A solitary walker on the nearby trail veers off course to get close to the gaggle. They eye him suspiciously and quickly waddle away. As I make my way to my bench, I approach the geese and laugh as they squawk and warn each other that potential danger is near. I must not seem terribly threatening, however, because most of the geese merely scurry away. Only a few take flight, flying about a hundred yards or so before landing on the frigid river.

The river is still flowing freely and not even a hint of ice has formed at its edges. We had the second snowfall of the season this week — less than an inch — and the ground is crusted with its icy remains. It's the same ice that has accumulated on my front steps. The first snowfalls of the season can be hazardous because they often melt quickly and turn to ice before the day is over. I've noticed that the "Minnesota Shuffle" has once again replaced our strong, confident gaits of warmer months.

Last year we received more than 89 inches of snow in the Twin Cities, the fourth highest amount since record-keeping began in 1871. Michelle Margraf, a meteorologist with the National Weather Service, says to brace for more of the same this year. Predictions call for above normal precipitation and below normal temperatures. This jibes with the forecast in the Old Farmers' Almanac, which warns of another cold, snowy winter.

Snow is welcomed by most this time of year because it beautifies the stark brown landscape and helps enhance the holiday spirit. Earlier this week I visited Rice Park to see the 65-foot-tall Christmas tree. I had read about how the tree trunk was inserted into a hole then surrounded by wooden wedges to hold it in place. I had to see it for myself and was amazed at how snuggly the lumber filled the space and how securely it held the tree in place.

It's my daughter's birthday today and I think of her as she now passes from her teens into her twenties. She is attending the University of Wisconsin-La Crosse, and I find it strangely comforting that the same river I'm looking at flows by her college town. I toss a birthday wish into the river and hope it finds her happy.

To my right I catch a glimpse of movement in the Pilot House suite of the Covington Inn, one of the few floating bed and breakfast establishments in the nation. I'm sure owner Liz Miller is thrilled to have a guest in the off-season. Last winter was challenging for her. Twice she awoke to frozen pipes and was forced to cancel reservations, resulting in lost income during her slowest time of the year. The Pilot House is encased in windows, and I'm sure its current resident is toasty warm. There's not a cloud in the sky to filter out the bright sunshine penetrating through.

On my way to the park I passed some maintenance men wrestling with a large sheet of plastic, which would be used to weatherproof one of the 22 boats of the live-aboard community that stays at the St. Paul Yacht Club year-round. I wonder how those residents cope with winter living in such close quarters.

The shipping season on the Mississippi is now over. On November 24, the MV Charlie G was the last commercial tow to pass through Lock and Dam #2 near Hastings. The river is much quieter now. Soon more snow will fall and frigid temps will form a cake of ice on the river. It's interesting to think about how each snowflake that floats down becomes part of the river, and to ponder where it will end up. Will it wash ashore in Red Wing? St. Louis? Or will it survive all the way to the Gulf of Mexico where it will cool the toes of some tourist on a beach in Mexico? I'd like to think the latter will happen, but that's because I'm cold now. My fingers are numb, as is my bottom from sitting on this hard metal bench.

My time is up. I'm off to find a bowl of soup.

January 6, 2012
12:30 p.m.
41 degrees F
Sunny

W hen I embarked on this project a few months ago one of the first images that came to mind was a cold bench in the middle of a wind-swept park blanketed with snow. At that time I knew what I would be wearing on this visit: long underwear, layers of clothing under a thick winter jacket, heavy socks and winter boots, and possibly a fleece facemask to protect my cheeks from the icy wind.

Today serves as a reminder of why I shouldn't worry about things over which I have no control, and to expect the unexpected. It is a balmy 41 degrees and sunny, more reminiscent of a fall day than one in the heart of winter. It brings to mind the classic scene in "White Christmas" when Bing and Danny step off the train in Vermont, bundled from head to toe, and are greeted by warm, sunny weather and a brown landscape.

Most people aren't complaining about the weather. The only ones undoubtedly frustrated are the folks organizing the Winter Carnival. It's hard to motivate people to celebrate our ability to embrace winter when we're running around without coats, and the warm weather makes it difficult to smugly thumb our nose at people like that New York reporter from 126 years ago who called St. Paul "another Siberia, unfit for human habitation in the winter." That comment gave birth to the Winter Carnival.

The river is still open and flowing freely. A few gulls are soaring overhead, which is an odd sight. I don't think I've ever seen gulls here in January. I'm sitting near the site where ferries used to transport people across the river before the many nearby bridges had been built. I can't imagine the amount of patience they had in those days to wait for a ferry to cross from the West Side into downtown St. Paul. Now, we have four bridges along a mile-and-a-half of St. Paul riverfront and we get frustrated if we have to wait for a red light.

The river means many things to many people. To some, it's a barrier that separates people and neighborhoods. To others, it's a ribbon of highway that leads to the sea. It also defines communities. For example, the people who live on the West Side have a tradition of living with the river, especially in the pre-floodwall days when it encroached on their homes in the springtime. It's a close-knit community and many of its residents refer to themselves as being "from St. Paul" only when they are outside of the Twin Cities. In the shadow of St. Paul's skyline, they proudly call themselves West Siders.

To my left, the riverfront trail through Harriet Island is paved with bricks, many of which are inscribed with names and messages. They were installed during the renovation of the park that began in the late 1990s. I get up and examine the line of bricks near my bench. They speak of community. One brick memorializes early settlers of St. Paul, another one a local congregation, and yet another a St. Paul cop. Many bricks contain surnames that reveal a melting pot of ancestries. The one from Kristi and Dennis is stamped with a special date, perhaps their first date, their wedding day or the birth of a child. Another brick has seven sets of initials, all ending with the letter W—a big, close family, no doubt. Bob and Linda's paver pledges "Now and Forever," while Ginny and Bill remind us that "Life is a Dance."

I read recently that a "not-to-be-missed Metro Mississippi adventure" is to walk over the Smith Avenue High Bridge. As I left the park, I decided to do just that. I've driven across the bridge hundreds of times but have never walked across it. I exited the park on Water Street, snaked my way up the bluff on Ohio Street, and turned right on Cherokee Avenue to reach a small park at the foot of the bridge.

The Cherokee Garden Club recognizes the importance of this place and beautifies it each year with a flower garden. Near the park is a sign that shows a sketch of the former High Bridge, which was imploded on February 25, 1985, and a sketch of the current bridge, completed in 1987. The sign is cracked and faded from withstanding 25 years of weather atop the bluff. The bridge is named after Robert Smith, a longtime St. Paul mayor who served in the late 1800s and early 1900s.

On the walkway, the view of the river and the skyline is stunning: iconic St. Paul. In one sweeping view you can see the large red "1" of the First National Bank sign, the domes of the St. Paul Cathedral and the State Capitol, mansions on the bluff and the Landmark Brewery sign.

Halfway across the bridge I stop and look over the edge to get a full view of the river, some 160 feet below. It's a majestic site to behold. Standing there with a gusty wind at my back, I couldn't help but think of the distraught people who have used this bridge to end their lives. The thought saddened me so I said a quick prayer for those of us who struggle that way that they can find hope.

Once across the bridge I saw the huge, green chair that welcomes people to the West Seventh neighborhood. I smiled because I immediately knew what I had to do to complete this urban adventure. I walked through a sandy area around the chair and crawled under the chair's large arm to climb aboard. The seat was covered with sand, so I am not the first in recent days to be on it. I brushed away the sand from the middle plank, sat down and took in the view of the High Bridge and a small portion of the river. I couldn't help laughing at myself. I felt small, like a child.

In the park near the chair is a pole inscribed in four languages: "May Peace Prevail on Earth."

Yes, may it be so.

The first thing I notice as I head to my bench is a puddle. That's right, a puddle in early February. It's a rare sight for this time of year, but not unusual for this winter given the near-record warm temps. This week it topped forty at least twice, resulting in only a few patches of snow left in the park, moving water in the river, and puddles.

Last weekend was colder, though. I took a hike in a park downriver where the Mississippi was mostly iced-over. I have kayaked this area several times and the waterfront for nearly six years, they have become walking and talking ambassadors of the city and the riverfront. When some friends were considering moving to Minneapolis recently Mary offered a tour of her home, combined with a tour of the city. They were hooked and signed a purchase agreement to become her neighbor.

It is people like Mary and Dianne that reinforce my belief that St. Paul is just one big small town. We spoke briefly and shared things we had in common, in particular a love of the river. At one point, Mary eyed me up and picked at the knee of my trousers.

"I know this is personal, but are you wearing underwear?"

I smiled. I knew she was referring to long underwear, and I assured her I was. Having read my past columns, she understands that spending a half-hour on a metal bench in the wintertime can be a chilling experience. She was happy to see that I was properly dressed for the weather. It was a conversation that would occur between friends. A conversation I was happy to have.

April 6, 2012
12:30 p.m.
61 degrees F
Sunny

The color green has returned to Harriet Island Regional Park. The great lawn is lush once again and is already in need of a trim. The stately cottonwoods that grace the park are bursting forth with foliage. Tiny heart-shaped leaves have sprouted from their buds, and their stringy seeds are dangling like fuzzy caterpillars next to them.

Children have also returned to the park. Several are swinging and sliding at the sandy playground, a few are kicking a soccer ball, and a boy is trying to fly a kite. He's struggling to get it to take flight, even

New Dog Park

Dog lovers have reason to be excited because the new High Bridge Dog Park is scheduled to open Memorial Day weekend. This fenced-in 7-acre parcel along the river on the former Xcel Energy power plant site offers an area for dog owners to recreate or train their dogs without a leash. A parking lot for the park is located near Shepard Road and Randolph Avenue.

Music in the Park

The sound of music will resonate through Harriet Island in June. St. Paul Parks and Recreation hosts summer concerts and movies at several parks throughout the city, including Raspberry Island, where you can feel the music pulsate through you as the river flows around you.

River Art

The American Veterans Memorial-Plaza de Honor, located at Harriet Island near the pavilion, is progressing nicely. It is the latest example of public art to grace the riverfront. St. Paul has many artists who create unique representations of the river and I was able to see a few of them this past weekend during the highly popular and well-attended St. Paul Art Crawl. Some of the studios in historic Lowertown have incredible views of the Mississippi River. Peering through their windows it's easy to see what inspires these artists.

My time is up and I'm hungry. The food trucks haven't started serving along Kellogg Boulevard yet—although they will start soon—so I'm heading to Lowertown. I know Joe or one of his guys will be hawking hot dogs on the corner of Sixth and Sibley. It will be a nice way to steal away a few more minutes in the sun.

friends who live in Hastings who make the nearly 80-mile round-trip trek to that bakery. At first it seems ridiculous that they would drive that far to get sweets. However, once you've traveled the river road and have breathed in the beauty of the countryside—and you understand that they are making the trip in their Mustang convertible, top down—you know it's an excellent idea.

Once I'm in Prescott, I'm back in familiar territory and am getting closer to home. The Great River Road runs directly in front of my house so I stay on it until my turn arrives. I'm guilty of traveling this road every day and not remembering its significance. However, on days like this one, when I slow down and appreciate my surroundings, I am reminded of how lucky I am to live where I do. I pull into my driveway feeling relaxed, refreshed and connected. The river valley is my home.

July 6, 2012
12:30 p.m.
96 degrees F
Overcast

It was bound to happen and today it did. As I walked across the great lawn at Harriet Island Regional Park I saw two young women sitting on my bench. I glanced around and could see a dozen other benches along the riverfront and they were all empty. Yet, they chose mine. I guess I can't blame them. It's a good bench. It is shaded by a large cottonwood tree and provides nice views of the river, both upstream and down.

I moved to a bench further on down the trail. At first I was disappointed but then I thought, *What the* day South St. Paul. The strongest hunters have a field-dressed deer slung over their shoulders while others are sharing the burden by carrying game that is lashed to a pole made from a freshly cut poplar tree. They are weary from the long, arduous hunt, but their spirits brighten when they see the faces of the villagers, filled with thankfulness from knowing they will eat well for many weeks ahead. In the evening, around the fire, the stories begin to spill from the hunting party and laughter fills the air. They talk of the difficulty of finding the game and of the hunters who demonstrated the most skill, and the ones with the least skill. They share tales of their prowess, as well as mishaps from their journey. The Indians in the Kaposia Village were known for their friendliness, hospitality and cosmopolitan ways. South St. Paul named its annual community celebration in honor of them, so their tribe is still remembered today.

I can see Robert Hickman, a former slave and preacher, floating hopelessly adrift on a raft on the Mississippi in Missouri in 1863. With him are 75 other slaves he is trying to lead to freedom. Their eyes are filled with worry and fear, knowing the fate that will befall them if they are discovered and returned to their "owners." Fortunately, they were discovered by the steamboat Northerner and towed to St. Paul, arriving on May 5, 1863. Hickman went on to found the Pilgrim Baptist Church in St. Paul and his heroic deeds are still retold to this day.

The day that Hickman and his followers arrived in St. Paul was exactly one year after the historic Battle of Puebla, where the Mexican Army defeated the more powerful French forces in its quest for independence. That day—Cinco de Mayo (May 5)—is celebrated annually in St. Paul by the large Hispanic community on the West Side, as is Mexican Independence Day, September 16. This community, and others who settled along the riverfront during the immigration boom of the last century, were displaced from their homes in 1962 when the city of St. Paul demolished the West Side Flats neighborhood, which was prone to constant flooding. The city eventually built a levee and an industrial park on their home sites, but the "Old West Side" is still remembered today.

I am thrust back to reality when a man in black shorts, a black t-shirt and sunglasses approaches me.

"Excuse me. Are you with the Irish Fair?" he asked politely.

"No," I replied.

"I'm sorry. I'm going to have to ask you to leave. The park is closed today for the Irish Fair."

I thought about protesting and telling him that the gatekeeper down the road told me it was OK to come into the park and that there were no signs announcing its closure. I thought about telling him I was with the media, assuming he would think I was there covering the event. However, I knew it was nearly time for me to go so I got up and told him I understood. I could tell that he wasn't happy about having to ask me to leave, and I knew he was likely doing it for my own safety. I walked away from my bench feeling fortunate that my feet didn't get run over by a vendor's vehicle, or by the snitch in the golf cart.

September 7, 2012
12:30 p.m.
68 degrees F
Overcast and breezy

Today the landscape looks like an oil painting. The river is reflecting the leaden hues of the large cloud bank lingering over it. Between the clouds are small patches of bright blue sky that are illuminating the edges of the clouds, giving them a surreal look. Even though it is breezy, the clouds are stationary. They look stubborn, like they are going to be around for awhile.

On September 22, the autumnal equinox arrives. Already, signs of fall are all around. The vegetation on the riverbank is no longer a lush, verdant green. Now it is speckled with muted amber tones and some of the foliage is already dead. Most of the trees, however, are still holding on to their summer appearance, but a few are suggesting a hint of autumn color.

I spoke with Gus at the Padelford Packetboat Company this week and he said they are busy booking their Fall Color Cruises, which are the most popular cruises of the year at the riverboat company based at Harriet Island. On the radio this week I also heard my first fall colors report. Cool temperatures and predicted frost in the north are threatening to force the change earlier than normal. Over the next few weeks it will work its way down to the metro area, which typically experiences peak colors in late September and early October.

People who take fall color cruises are those among us who take the time to marvel at the splendor of nature and the change in seasons, and the Mississippi River Valley rarely disappoints. Many of us see the river every day, but I wonder how many of us actually *see* the river. Has it become commonplace?

Mark Twain struggled with this conundrum. In chapter 9 of his autobiographical work, "Life on the Mississippi," he penned a splendid little essay on "Two Ways of Seeing a River." As a young man, Twain aspired to become a great steamboat pilot. In order to do that, he was forced to study every aspect of the river and get to know it intimately. Once he "mastered the language of the water," however, he lamented that he was a changed man. "I had lost something that could never be restored to me while I lived," he wrote. "All the grace, the beauty, the poetry had gone out of the majestic river!"

I'm thankful that we have poets and artists to remind us of the beauty of nature. St. Paul is home to many artists who capture the beauty of the river. You may view their work during the semi-annual St. Paul Art Crawl, held in April and October. One of the hundreds of artists who will open their doors to the public this fall is Tom McGregor. He has a studio in Historic Lowertown and has painted several landscapes of the Mississippi River, including "Saint Paul at Dawn." In an artist's statement on the painting he writes, "After 23 years of living in St. Paul, I still get a thrill from its old buildings and bridges along the mighty Mississippi. The bluffs surrounding the city on three sides afford the viewer unrivaled panoramas." He sees the beauty of the river and is able to capture it on canvas.

Sitting on my bench, I see a few leaves skittering across the paved trail. I reach down, pick one up and examine it. It is brown and brittle, with visible veins that have been sucked dry of all that once gave it life. I crumple it between my fingers, smell its aroma, then let the small flakes scatter in the wind. Walking back to my truck, I playfully step on as many downed leaves as possible. The crunch I hear beneath my feet tells me that fall has indeed arrived.

October 5, 2012
12:30 p.m.
41 degrees F
Cloudy and windy

The weather this week has been glorious, up until Wednesday, that is. It was then that a cold front moved in and chased away the sun and warm temps that have graced us over the past several weeks. No one is complaining, though. Our neighbors in the northland received nearly a foot of snow yesterday, leaving us in the Twin Cities feeling like we've dodged a bullet.

I was hoping for a more temperate time for my last outing on my bench. According to the Old Farmer's Almanac, the first weekend in October nearly always has good weather. But that's life, so here I sit, feeling the cold steel of the bench through my trousers, the wind stinging my ears. My first thoughts are *why didn't I dress warmer; why didn't I bring a stocking cap?*

The river is dark, choppy and moving swiftly, pushed along by a strong westerly breeze. Many of the trees around me have ripened red and gold. Park users are few and far between, yet people occasionally happen by. Most are either walking or running. One couple is sitting on the opposite bank gazing at the river, huddled close together. I can't tell if they are talking or not. They look inanimate to me.

As I think back over the past 12 months I feel fortunate that I picked the year that I did for this exercise. While on my bench, it was never colder than 31 degrees and never warmer than 96 degrees. The average temperature was 60 degrees. That's not to say I wasn't cold or hot, because I was both. I sat in the wind and the rain and the snow, was forced to sit on a different bench once, and was even kicked off my bench and out of the park. During my time here, I've seen scores of people using the park and the river for recreation and commerce: walkers, runners, bikers, sunbathers, fishermen, boaters, public safety personnel and riverboat pilots. It's been an enjoyable experience, yet questions swirl around in my mind: what have I learned from it? Why are people drawn to the river? Why am I drawn to the river?

I think it has to do with a feeling of connectedness. Since the advent of time, people have settled along rivers. It can be argued that it has been for practical purposes — navigation, fertile land and the like — but I think it also has to do with our need to be connected to the land, to nature, and to each other. The Mississippi River is like no other in the United States. It is massive and bisects our country, touching 10 states and traveling over 2,300 miles through the heartland of our nation. Those of us who live near it rarely feel the need to call it by its given name. We simply refer to it as "The River." It's our river. It stitches our nation together like a giant piece of thread. It is strong and steady and rarely changes.

When I look at the river from my bench, I know this to be true. It looks the same as it did a year ago. Very little has changed around it. Then I glance at the bridges that bookend the park — the Smith Avenue High Bridge and the Wabasha Street Bridge. The cars that stream along these bridges remind me that there is much happening in the world around me. We are a few weeks away from making some important decisions regarding our State Constitution and our elected officials at every level of government. It is comforting to know that one can always come to the river to relax and reflect.

Tall Tales of the Big River

Hustlers, swindlers, explorers and industrialists — the Mississippi River has seen them all. They are the eclectic and sorted individuals that fill the pages of the book of one of the mightiest rivers in the world, and the characters that add to the aura and mystique of the Father of Waters.

Since people have been moving on its waters, the Mississippi River has been the source of tall tales and legends. From fish the size of small submarines to the spray of gangsters' bullets, St. Paul's stretch of the river has its share of stories to tell: many strange, colorful and oftentimes true. Two local historians — Stephen Lee and Lois Glewwe — have individually compiled a great source of local Mississippi River history. Lee's work is published in the Mississippi River Field Guide, found on the Friends of the Mississippi River website (www.fmr.org); Glewwe's in a number of local city history books, including "South St. Paul Centennial, 1887-1987: The History of South St. Paul, Minnesota."

Here are some of the most interesting tales they recount:

A Miraculous High Wire Act

According to Lee's sources, on January 22, 1962, a driver lost control of his vehicle while traveling across the Smith Avenue High Bridge in St. Paul, a bridge that is 160 feet above the water. The vehicle plunged off the bridge and tumbled toward the icy water below. However, it landed upside down on a telephone line, sprung back into the air, flipped over and landed upright on all four wheels, with no injuries to its passengers. No mention if the driver called for a ride home, or if the phone lines were down, making it impossible.

The Death of a Chief

Glewwe has written much about the Kaposia Band of the Dakota Indians, the first inhabitants along the river in what is now South St. Paul. Her writings preserve a tragic and bizarre accident of one of its chiefs. In the fall of 1845, Big Thunder was walking up a winding path near present-day Bryant Avenue in South St. Paul. He was strolling along behind his horse cart, being driven by one of his wives. As the cart bumped along on the dusty trail, his rifle, which was pointed toward him, began to slide off the cart. He reached out to grab it but the gun discharged, inflicting a wound that led to his death.

Don't Drink the Water...or Do

While much of our drinking water comes from the Mississippi River, few would dare to dip a cup in its current and raise it to his or her lips. That might not have been the case in 1921 for those looking to quench their thirst during the height of Prohibition. According to Lee's sources, in October of that year, federal agents and local police were busy raiding moonshiners' camps, many of which were hidden away among the forested banks of the river and on its islands. During one island raid, the authorities found a camp with 450 gallons of corn mash, which they dumped in the river. No mention if the speakeasies closed early that night for a party along the river.

When the Past and Future Collide

Little else conjures up romantic images of the Mississippi River more so than the steamboat, those lumbering, multi-decked ships that churned the river, belching out thick black smoke and blowing their distinctive whistles. The first to arrive in present day St. Paul was the Virginia, on May 10, 1823. Less than 100 years later, steamboats were becoming obsolete due to rail traffic. According to Glewwe's sources, a tragic accident occurred in 1912 that would fortell the fact that steamboats and trains would never coexist.

On the foggy evening of October 15, 1912, engineer Charles Kramer approached a swing-bridge downriver from St. Paul, his engine pulling along eight cars filled with livestock. The Hiawatha was steaming on the river nearby and was passing through the bridge, which was opened for her. The pilot heard the thunderous clamor of the train and quickly realized that it wasn't slowing down, so he sounded his whistle in warning. Unfortunately, Kramer did not hear it and he and his train plunged into the river, killing him in the process.

Today, the river continues to be a source of our conversation and imagination. It sees our worst—from people drowning in it to people ending another's life in it—but it also sees our best, from people working to protect it for future generations to those who give generously of their time to hold back flood waters to protect their neighbors' lives and property. It's their deeds that inspire our folk history and our legends.

People still sit around in their living rooms telling stories of boating mishaps, fishing and hunting trophies, and times when they were knee-deep in the rising river filling sandbags. School children still study the lives of those who first explored and settled the Upper Mississippi. Others share tales about some of the region's most colorful characters, including Pierre "Pig's Eye" Parrant, a moonshiner for whom the village that is today the city of St. Paul was first named, and Jane Robinson, a federal light keeper who rowed more than 50,000 miles in her career to tend the kerosene lamps that lighted the way for riverboat pilots in St. Paul from 1885 to 1921. The Mississippi is an ever-present source of adventure. If you've spent any amount of time exploring it, you likely have a few tall tales of your own.

PART III

EXPLORING
the Mississippi National
River and Recreation Area

Walking in One Man's Legacy

December 2012

I'm standing on a small spit of land at the far western edge of Harriet Island Regional Park and am surrounded by the legacy of a man whom I have never met nor will ever have the opportunity to meet. A plaque in front of me pays homage to the man: Tom Kelley, credited by many as being the pioneer of riverfront renewal efforts in the Twin Cities.

As I gaze at the plaque, my surroundings and the river softly lapping at the shoreline, I marvel at the thought of what can happen when one man dares to cast a vision for the future. Kelley, who passed away in 2007, is remembered as an advocate who worked tirelessly to preserve the river corridor in the Twin Cities for future generations. His words, inscribed on the plaque, aptly sum up his beliefs about the river: "It's one big river. It belongs to everybody."

I can imagine him standing in this same spot over 25 years ago, undoubtedly thinking thoughts much different than mine today. At that time the water was murky brown and highly polluted. Today the river is odor-free and cleaner than it's been in decades. A report released this fall shows that pollution is down considerably and that game fish, mussels and bald eagles have rebounded significantly. The landscape around him in those days was also in need of help. Now, invasive vegetation has been removed from the park, and native trees and shrubbery, many planted from 1999 to 2009 during the renovation of Harriet Island, are thriving. Nearby is a massive cottonwood tree that has witnessed the rise, fall and rebirth of this park. The tree has so much girth that it would take six average-sized men clasping their hands together to encompass it.

If Kelley were alive today I am sure he would be thrilled with the renaissance of the MNRRA corridor, particularly with what has occurred at Harriet Island Regional Park. This park truly is the poster child for recreational riverfront development. In 1988 it was a rather scrubby park with a chain link fence separating it from the river. Today it features picnic shelters, a restored pavilion, a riverfront trail, a great lawn, public dock, band shells and more. Thousands visit the park each year to ride the Padelford Riverboats. They were not here 25 years ago. People are also able to see a play on the Centennial Showboat or spend a romantic evening on the river at the Covington Inn Bed and Breakfast, two other unique amenities that were absent when MNRRA was formed.

Kelley spent his early career as a journalist in Chicago, Washington, D.C. and the Twin Cities. However, he felt called to a life of public service so he abandoned his early ambitions and dove into government work, where he served at the state, county and city levels. In 1966, he was appointed Ramsey County auditor and quickly began to use his influence to bring about change along the riverfront. He went on to serve as county executive for Ramsey County and city administrator for the city of St. Paul. In addition, he was a commissioner on the Mississippi River Corridor Commission, which established the framework for MNRRA. After he retired in 1984, the area I'm now standing in was named Kelley's Landing in his honor. It was eventually renamed Kelley's Overlook. It's a special spot for Kelley's family and friends. After his death, his ashes were sprinkled in the river just upstream from the overlook.

While it's important to honor the legacy that Kelley helped create, it's also vital to remember that numerous others were involved in the process in the early days, and that many others are still planning and working to bring about more improvements in the

MNRRA corridor. Some 20 municipalities are linked by the Mississippi River and continue to develop their portion of the riverfront as well. Today, the Mill City Museum and Guthrie Theater in Minneapolis are examples of new and improved cultural amenities on the riverfront. From the confluence of the Crow River at the northern end of the corridor to the Vermillion River flood plain at the southern boundary, more parks are being developed every year, more miles of trails are being paved and more access points and interpretive sites are being created. Every mile of the MNRRA corridor offers a new adventure for those who choose to explore it.

Tasty Traditions along the Mississippi River

January 2013

I've enjoyed spicy gumbo and a shrimp-stuffed Po' boy sandwich on a sultry summer evening in the French Quarter in New Orleans and had mouth-watering barbeque ribs in St. Louis, for which I waited in a long serpentine line for over 90 minutes to order, and was fortunate to be on the inside looking out when they taped a sign to the window that said "out of meat," but my food experiences along the river in the Twin Cities have left much to be desired. There are countless restaurants in the MNRRA corridor that offer tasty fare for all palates and pocketbooks, so I set out to find a unique dining experience, one I could proudly recommend to an out-of-town visitor.

My quest led me to the internet, where I discovered that the Dakota, a world-class jazz club and restaurant in Minneapolis, hosts Foodie Nights, featuring a local jazz musician and a sampler menu. *Perfect*, I thought. There is no musical genre more associated with the river than jazz, and a quick peek at the Dakota's online menu revealed that I could sample items I've never before had the courage to try.

The Dakota was established in 1985 at Bandana Square in St. Paul but relocated in 2003 to its present location at 1010 Nicollet Ave. in downtown Minneapolis. The Twin Cities have a long love affair with this truly American art form. Jazz was birthed in the South in the early 20th century and worked its way up the river on steamboats. It slowly filtered into saloons along the Lower Landing in St. Paul and then to other locales in the Twin Cities.

My evening began by viewing the menu, which was tucked inside an album cover: "The Fabulous Philadelphia Sound Series." I admit that I'm a bit of a foodie neophyte, made evident by the fact that there were numerous items on the menu that I've never tried, and some of which I couldn't pronounce. I chose the Day Boat Scallops, served with potato pavé, wild mushroom, mebrillo, micro green salad and truffle. It was all delicious, especially the rich, tender scallops. I enjoyed my meal with a glass of white wine and ate slowly, savoring each scrumptious bite. For dessert I had the pear tart, made with candied walnuts, citrus-ricotta custard, pickled pears and lemon crème fraîche. When it arrived, it looked too beautiful to eat. Eventually, I put a fork to it and brought it to my lips. The sweet, tart taste exploded in my mouth and a wave of delight washed over me.

Following dinner I waited patiently for Sophia Shorai to take the stage. Shorai, a classically trained pianist who started performing at age nine, gravitated toward jazz in her early teens. She was raised in Minneapolis and is a regular performer at the Dakota, although her performance calendar boasts nearly 100 dates a year at venues around the Twin Cities. She superbly covered many tunes, as well as some originals soon to be released on her newest CD.

After the performance, I drove to the riverfront and strolled out on the historic Stone Arch Bridge, which railroad tycoon James J. Hill built in 1883 to get his Great Northern Railroad from one side of the river to the other as it chugged its way out west. The last train crossed in 1978, seven years after the bridge was added to the National Register of Historic Places. Following its closure, it slowly faded into disrepair. In the early 1990s it was renovated for pedestrian and bicycle use.

As I walked out on the bridge the cacophony of city noise filled the dark, cloudy night. I tuned it out and recalled the performance I'd just witnessed, the throaty vocals, the tickling of ivory, the fingering of fat cello strings, the soft brushing of a snare drum. Standing in the middle of the bridge, I looked upstream and could make out the shadow of the river as it rushed over the spillway toward St. Paul, and St. Louis, and New Orleans. I closed my eyes and heard the rush of the water and envisioned the river two hundred years ago when it ran wild through this place and dropped over 50 feet through a series of falls and rugged rapids. I looked downstream and saw the new I-35W bridge, which replaced the one that collapsed in 2007. The underside of the bridge is illuminated by a series of LED light fixtures that allow nearly any color to be cast upon it. This night it reflected a soft neon blue. I looked at it and thought, *Man, that's cool. It's blue. Like jazz.*

Searching for Hiawatha and Minnehaha

February 2013

There is a small tributary of the Mississippi River that takes its breath from Lake Minnetonka and meanders 22 miles through the backyards of suburban and urban homes before it exhales into the river. It is likely the most famous of all streams in the Mississippi National River and Recreation Area, most notable for the 53-foot-high waterfall that bears its name: Minnehaha.

The falls are the signature attraction of Minnehaha

Regional Park, located along the Mississippi River near the intersection of Hiawatha Avenue and Minnehaha Parkway in South Minneapolis. More than 1.2 million people flock to the park annually to gaze upon the majestic falls. I have been among the summer throngs but have never viewed the falls when they are gripped by the hand of winter. I decided to visit them when the solstice moon waxed on one side of a new year and waned on the other.

As I planned my adventure, I realized I didn't know much about the lore behind their namesake so I purchased a copy of "The Song of Hiawatha" by Henry Wadsworth Longfellow. It was my intention to read the poem while sitting near the falls. Once I got my copy, I knew that wouldn't happen. The poem is oft referred to as epic, not only for its content but also for its length: 256 pages. Rather than take the risk of having someone find me frozen to a bench with Longfellow's masterpiece in hand, I chose instead to read it in the comfort of my home over the course of a week. Reading classic literature beside a crackling fire is an enjoyable way to wile away the longest nights of the year.

"The Song of Hiawatha" was published in 1855 and weaves together the folklore and myths of the Native Americans who first occupied this land. Longfellow drew much of his research for the poem from the writings of Henry Rowe Schoolcraft, who extensively studied Native American cultures. Schoolcraft passed through this area in 1824 and again in 1832 on his famous expedition to discover the source of the Mississippi River.

I visited the falls twice recently: first when I purchased a copy of the poem, and then after I had read it. On my first trip I marveled at what freezing temps can do to the outflow of a tiny creek that plunges off a 53-foot high precipice. That day the falls were a half-moon of a hundred columns of jagged blue ice and were indeed an awe-inspiring sight. A tiny trickle of water bubbled from them and quickly retreated beneath the crust of ice that covered the creek. I followed the frozen stream about a half-mile through the wooded ravine until I reached its confluence with the Mississippi River. As I stood on the shoulder of ice near the open water of the river I could envision Hiawatha making his solitary way through the valley.

It wasn't until my return visit that I truly understood the significance of this area to Native Americans. On that day I paid little attention to the falls because I was more interested in the life-size bronze statue of Hiawatha and Minnehaha that is perched on a tiny island in the creek just upstream from the falls. Hiawatha is carrying his lover in his arms, his right leg outstretched, toes pointed down, as he is ready to enter the stream. He and Minnehaha are both looking at the stream as if pondering the distinct danger of slipping and being swept over the falls. Nonetheless, the young Hiawatha appears confident and virile. He has "crossed the Mighty Mississippi" to the "land of the Dakotahs, where the falls of Minnehaha Flash and gleam among the oak trees, laugh and leap into the valley" to take Minnehaha back to the "shore of Gitche Gumme, by the shining Big-Sea-Water." This statue captures the heart of a couple just beginning their lives together, with vast possibilities before them. They don't know what the future has in store for them but they are determined to carve out a life together and leave their mark on the world. And they know that sharing their journey together will make it that much better, come what may.

Romancing the River

March 2013

In late March the first towboats of the season will be slowly pushing barges into the St. Paul harbor. Watching the vessels maneuver around the river bends and through the locks is a favorite pastime for many in the Mississippi National River and Recreation Area. I enjoy this as well and have often wondered what it would be like to live aboard one of the tows. One has two options to experience this: hire on as a deckhand or visit the Covington Inn, a floating bed and breakfast moored at Harriet Island Regional Park.

After reading the job description of a deckhand from one of the local tow companies I decided the lifestyle is not overly appealing. A deckhand spends much of his time doing dull maintenance duties, inside and out. They are required to clean the living quarters of the captain, pilot and engineer, including making their beds and cleaning their bathrooms, and they also help clean the galley, wash dishes and dirty linens and take out the trash.

The Covington Inn, on the other hand, boasts that it treats its customers like a tow company VIP. Each of its four unique private staterooms has a comfortable bed, a private bath, fireplace, nautical fixtures, antiques and historic art. Innkeeper Liz Miller takes care of all the housekeeping chores and serves up a delicious gourmet breakfast for her guests.

The Covington was built in 1946 and was used for 30 years to push barges along a 1,000-mile stretch of the Ohio and Mississippi rivers. In 1976, members of the River Valley Preservation Company found it in dry dock in Louisiana and made arrangements to purchase it and bring it to St. Paul for restoration. In 1995, it became one of the country's first floating bed and breakfast venues. Miller has owned it for nine years.

Two weeks before Valentine's Day, I called to reserve a room for my wife and me. I was hoping to book the Pilot House, a two-room suite on the upper deck with a 360-degree view, but it was taken, as were the Mate's Quarters and the Master's Quarters. The Riverview Suite, a private room below deck, was available so I quickly snatched it up.

Our evening began by visiting three neighboring establishments. First we visited the new Tap Room at the Summit Brewery, 910 Montreal Circle, St. Paul, located on the bluff overlooking the river. The Tap Room, which has an outdoor patio for summer use, serves a line-up of Summit beers every Friday, 3-8 p.m. We were hoping to get a pint of Winter Ale, but they were out. The bartender said this seasonal favorite is a hot seller. Rather than be disappointed, I took it as a good sign that spring is on its way. On tap were Maibock, a spring seasonal, and eight to 10 other beers.

We each ordered a flight so we could sample four varieties, and found a seat at the long rows of lunchroom style tables. The crowd was lively and eclectic, featuring a mix of nearly every demographic category you can imagine: age, gender, race, etc. A deejay was spinning vinyl on a turntable and patrons were engaged in conversation or in one of the games they pulled off a shelf, such as backgammon, cards and Guess Who.

About halfway through our flight I saw Mark Stutrud enter and start mingling with the crowd. Stutrud founded the company in 1986 and continues to direct its future. He had his coat on, his briefcase draped over his shoulder and a beer in hand. It looked like he just punched out and was spending time with his friends before going home.

From there, we went to Mancini's Char House on West Seventh Street. Mancini's is one of the oldest family-owned restaurants in the MNRRA corridor, established in 1948. This St. Paul dining institution is known for its mouth-watering steaks and lobsters that are charbroiled to perfection over open hearth charcoal pits. Mancini's holds the aura of supper clubs of days of yore. We waited nearly 45 minutes for our table, but we were able to do so in a comfortable booth in the lounge. The steaks were worth the wait and we agreed they were likely the best we'd ever had.

On our way back to the Covington we stopped at Candyland in downtown St. Paul. While much of St. Paul goes dark after 5 p.m., this business does not. It is open until 10 p.m., Monday through Saturday, and until 9 p.m. on Sunday. Candyland opened in 1932 on Wabasha Street under the name "Flavocorn," selling unique varieties of popcorn. It has changed hands twice, in 1938 and then in 1981 when current owners Doug and Brenda Lamb purchased it.

Once you visit the store it's difficult to choose which treat to purchase. The tantalizing scent of popcorn first tempts your senses, but then you see the handmade chocolates drying on nearby cooling racks. Soon, their aroma wafts around you and clouds your judgment. We purchased a half dozen different chocolate creations and took them back to the Covington to savor with a bottle of wine that we purchased this fall from one of the wineries on the Great River Wine Trail in southeastern Minnesota. The chocolate and wine were a delight and we enjoyed them in our cozy suite while gazing at a warm, glowing fire, the lights of the city visible through our portholes. We raised our glasses and toasted a wonderful evening.

The next morning we lingered aboard the boat. Breakfast was served at 9 a.m. in the main salon, which features dining tables, comfortable furniture, a small library with books on the river, and awesome views of the river and the St. Paul skyline. We chatted with the other guests and with Miller, who kept glancing out the windows to watch the eagles, her favorite part of living on the river. We joined her in watching them soar overhead and swoop down to the river's surface looking for their own breakfast. The responsibilities of our day lay before us but they seemed far away and insignificant as we leisurely sipped coffee while admiring the river in its quiet, frozen form.

Noteworthy Viewpoints of the River

April 2013

few years ago the U.S. Army Corps of Engineers uncovered an album of photographs of the Mississippi River that today is valued at $4.5 million. The remarkable collection was taken by Henry Peter Bosse, who documented the work of the Corps along the Upper Mississippi from 1883 to 1892. The images show the Corps in action as it reshaped the river for commercial navigation, but several of them also capture scenic vistas that have since been significantly altered by modern development or have disappeared altogether from the landscape.

One of my favorite Bosse images was taken in 1891, in Nininger Township near Hastings. It shows a man sitting in a grassy meadow atop a steep bluff. He is dressed in slacks, white shirt and suspenders, and top hat. His hands are grasping his knees as he looks out across the river, which spreads out wide before him before disappearing into the horizon. The man isn't identified, yet we can relate to him and imagine what he is experiencing at that moment in time. Who among us who loves the river hasn't sat contentedly on a scenic vista and stared at the river? Such overlooks offer a sanctuary at which we can pause, reflect and contemplate life.

The National Park Service recognizes the value of scenic overlooks and is working to preserve more of them in the MNRRA corridor. As part of its Visual Resource Protection Plan, the Park Service has recently solicited public comments on favorite scenic viewpoints in the corridor. Nearly 100 people have weighed in on their favorites. If given the chance, people are quick to share their opinions. It's an age-old habit of celebrating the places we love. In a chapter in "Life on the Mississippi" entitled Legends and Scenery, Mark Twain recounts a conversation with an old man who bragged incessantly about the scenery on the Upper Mississippi, sometimes "slamming in a three-ton word" to illustrate his point. Twain said he was glad to hear his description of the scenery, "for it assisted my appreciation of what I saw of it."

The National Park Service's map of MNRRA has seven scenic overlooks denoted by a simple black dot. I decided to visit each of them to note their significance and see if any are worthy of a three-ton word.

Cloquet Scenic Overlook - Located in Dayton at the northern end of the corridor, this overlook has limited views of the river, but what you can see of it is beautiful and wild. Looking through a mixture of pines and hardwoods, you can see the river as it wraps around Cloquet Island. Graffiti on the handrail summed up one viewer's opinion. It said, "Minnesota is nice," and had an arrow pointing toward the river.

Coon Rapids Dam Overlook - I nearly omitted visiting this location because it was on a dam site, but I'm glad I went because it offers a unique opportunity to stand in the middle of the river. Looking upstream, the river is placid and tranquil. Looking downstream, one can see the powerful flow of water thundering over the dam. It spills out near Coon Island, which is said to have some of the most wild and diverse habitat in the entire corridor.

Stone Bridge Arch Overlook - This overlook is the most urban and historic. Here the river is engulfed within the city of Minneapolis. Its banks are lined with remnants of the city's industrialist past as the milling center of the world, as well as its present day commerce. At St. Anthony Falls you can also see the first lock on the river.

Mississippi River Gorge Overlook - Located near Summit and Mississippi River boulevards in St. Paul, this overlook offers the best vista of the beautiful gorge. Looking at the river and surrounding landscape from this vantage point it's impossible to tell that you are just minutes from both downtowns of the Twin Cities. A bonus of this overlook is that it is close to Shadow Falls, a picturesque waterfall that carves a deep ravine toward the river.

Vento View Overlook - This overlook was named in honor of the late Bruce Vento, a U.S. Congressman from Minnesota who was instrumental in initiating a study that ultimately led to the creation of MNRRA. The trailhead is located near the entrance of Cherokee Regional Park, near Highway 13 and Annapolis. From there, it's a short hike through the wooded bluff line to reach the secluded overlook. Vento's View overlooks Pickerel Lake and offers a panoramic view of the river valley, including the skylines of St. Paul and Minneapolis.

Mounds Park Overlook - This overlook offers the best view of the river as part of our overall transportation network, as well as St. Paul's skyline. Looking out, one can see all forms of competing transportation methods, including auto and truck traffic, airplanes taking off and landing at nearby Holman Field, freight trains, and barges on the river.

Spring Lake Park Overlook - This overlook is located in Spring Lake Park Reserve near Hastings. To reach it you walk along a paved path high atop a bluff that offers sweeping views of the river around Grey Cloud Island. The view at the overlook is partially obstructed by trees. However, gaps in the tree line allow you to see both upstream and down. This is one of the best overlooks for those seeking solitude.

It is difficult to say which of the overlooks is the most scenic, for each has its own unique attributes and interprets a different aspect of the river. I conclude that each is — warning: three-ton word ahead — splendiferous in its own way. It's a worthy goal of the Park Service to create more overlooks in the corridor and I look forward to viewing the river from them as they are established.

Bosse Collection

Bosse's photographs have been digitized by the Minnesota Historical Society and may be viewed at http://reflections.mndigital.org/cdm/landingpage/collection/army

Welcoming the Return
of the Color Green

May 2013

The return of the color green to the riverfront is like balm to the soul of the weary masses inflicted by the wounds of winter. It's a magical phenomenon that happens each spring when the sun hangs around longer in the sky and when cleansing rains rinse and scour the earth. The first hints of it are detected only by eyes that are looking for it. It appears on the deciduous undergrowth on the southern slopes that devour the largest amounts of nourishing sunshine. Tender buds drop their scales and burst forth tiny shoots, creating a soft emerald haze along the riverbank. In a matter of weeks, all vegetation has been revived, and inevitably one weekend in May everything pops, and leaves from even the tallest trees unfurl and wave to us from branches above.

Recently, I set out in search of this marvel with my eyes wide open. I went on my green-seeking journey on a funky looking neon green bike offered through the NiceRide bike-sharing program. I had yet to rent one of these bikes and this seemed a fitting opportunity to do so. The program began in June 2010 and has since attracted 575,000 riders who have hopped on the bikes for both recreational and commuting purposes. Today, more than 1,500 bikes are offered at 170 locations in St. Paul and Minneapolis. They are available 24 hours a day, seven days a week from April to November. For more information, visit www.niceridemn.org.

The National Park Service is a sponsor of the program and has funded more than 50 stations. In late February, it received a $504,000 grant to install 17 new stations in north Minneapolis. The grant is part of the Federal Transit Administration's Transit in Parks program that is providing $12.5 million for 29 projects in 20 states to improve access to America's national parks, forests and wildlife refuges.

I rented my bike from the Harriet Island station on Water Street. It was easy to do. I simply swiped my credit card at the pay station, printed out a code and entered it into one of the bike docks. A light flashed green and I retrieved my bike. The rental rate is $6, which allows patrons to use a bike for up to 30 minutes. If you keep the bike longer, additional fees apply. However, if you return it to another station within 30 minutes, you can use the code to unlock a different bike without paying another fee. This can happen an unlimited number of times during a 24-hour period.

I hopped on the bike and cruised around Harriet Island, Raspberry Island and into Lilydale Regional Park. The bikes have wide, comfortable seats and are easy to ride but are not intended for high speed. They have just three gears, which aptly served my needs for the relatively flat terrain I traveled.

The trail through Lilydale Park runs directly along the river and offers great views of the river, the Smith Avenue High Bridge and the St. Paul skyline. I rode past the St. Paul Yacht Club wondering if I would see any boaters there, but saw only mallards and gulls gently bobbing up and down in the slips. I was happy that the waterfowl had returned to join other birds that have recently migrated back. In the past week I've seen numerous robins, juncos and other birds, and been treated to a melodious symphony on my morning walks.

On the steep bluff on the south side of the road through Lilydale Park I saw three small waterfalls, all still encased in snow and ice. The landscape around me was brown and barren and I thought my prospect of finding greenery would be for naught. Then I slowed down and stopped. I leaned over my handlebar and peered deeply into the underbrush along the river and spotted a few tufts of green grass, and then some bright green leaves on spindly ground cover. I smiled. It wasn't much, but it was enough, for I knew that more would soon follow.

A National Park with Benefits

June 2013

I've had the privilege of exploring more than a
dozen national parks and recreation areas. Many
of these visits have been with my close friend,
Tharren. I met Tharren in eighth grade and we became
instant friends. Our bond strengthened during high
school and continues to this day, thanks, in part, to our
annual backcountry adventures. After we started our
families, we coerced our wives into letting us take a few
days each year to travel to the most scenic areas in the
country to climb mountains, run rivers and hike trails.
Through career changes, the birth of seven kids—four
for me, three for him—we've never missed a trip.

An interesting phenomenon occurs on the final leg of each of our backcountry journies. It happens when we're trudging down a trail trying to force ourselves to ignore the aching pain in our tired feet, and the weight of a 60-pound pack digging into our shoulders. Conversation is non-existent at this point, but we are both thinking the same thing: where we will eat our celebration meal when we get off the trail and back to civilization. The thought of sizzling steaks, dry-rub ribs slathered in BBQ sauce, and fresh baked pizzas have made the final miles of every trip possible.

The advantage of exploring the Mississippi National River and Recreation Area is that you are never far from a great restaurant. Whether you are canoeing or kayaking the river, or hiking, biking or running a trail, the options for a meal to reward yourself for your accomplishment are endless.

This spring, my thoughts turned toward outdoor dining, so I did some research, made a list and recently set out to explore the options for riverfront dining. Here are the restaurants I visited that offer a patio with a view of the river.

Psycho Suzie's Motor Lounge
1900 Marshall St., N.E., Minneapolis
612-788-9069; www.psychosuzis.com
Vibe: Eclectic

If you're looking for a unique place to enjoy a good meal and a rum-infused libation, Psycho Suzie's is the place for you. Inside this tiki bar you'll find a waterfall, ferns, tiki wood furniture and three themed bars: the Shrunken Head, Forbidden Cove and Ports of Pleasure. Outside is the largest patio of any of the restaurants I visited. It overlooks the river and an industrial site. The restaurant boasts "world famous" pizzas and tiki drinks "served in tacky mugs with stupid garnishes for you to ponder and enjoy. And for an extra lousy $5 you can keep the mug." I knew the atmosphere was as relaxed and casual as it appeared when my tattooed waitress approached me and said, "What'll it be, dude?"

St. Anthony Main
Main Street at Central Avenue, Minneapolis
Vibe: Urban hip

Of our sister cities, Minneapolis has the upper hand on riverfront dining. Six restaurants with patio dining are located along a three-block area at the historic St. Anthony Main. The district features charming brick and stone buildings dating to the 1850s, a cobblestone street adjacent to the river, a paved trail, and summer concerts.

To work up an appetite, or work off your meal, you can stroll along the 1.8-mile trail that takes you along the Mississippi River and past Nicollet Island and the Hennepin Avenue and Stone Arch bridges. If you'd prefer to pedal the trail, a NiceRide bike rental station is located in the center of the district. Also available are Segway tours, trolley rides and horse-drawn carriage rides. Restaurants include:

Wilde Roast Cafe
65 Main St. S.E., Minneapolis
612-331-4544; www.wilderoastcafe.com

The Wilde Roast Cafe bills itself as "a neighborhood restaurant with an updated Victorian theme." It is named after Oscar Wilde, the popular 19th century author.

Aster Cafe
125 Main St. S.E., Minneapolis
612-379-3138; www.aster-cafe.com

The locally owned Astor features live music on the weekends.

Vic's
201 Main St. S.E., Minneapolis
612-310-2000; www.vicsminneapolis.com

Vic's is open for dinner only. It's the most upscale restaurant in the district and features a 99-bottle wine menu.

Tuggs Tavern
219 Main St. S.E., Minneapolis
612-379-4404; www.tuggsminneapolis.com

Tuggs takes its theme from "the great riverboat days of the Mighty Mississippi" and specializes in unique burgers.

Nicollet Island Inn
95 Merriam St., Minneapolis
612-331-1800; www.nicolletislandinn.com

The Nicollet Island Inn has the smallest patio of any I visited, but the restaurant is one of the most widely recognized, drawing reviews from regional and national publications for "Best Brunch," "Best View" and "Most Romantic Dining."

St. Paul Riverfront
Vibe: Casual

If you're looking for patio dining along the river in St. Paul, you'll be looking a long time because it doesn't exist. It's a shame that the city doesn't have at least one restaurant with riverfront patio dining. However, if it's any consolation, it is in the city's master plan for riverfront development to attract one or more restaurants for this purpose.

Your best bet for riverfront dining is to grab an entree from the mobile food court at Kellogg Park at Kellogg and Robert streets in downtown St. Paul and sit on the lawn overlooking the river. Food and live music are offered 11 a.m.-2 p.m. every Thursday through August. This year vendors are providing picnic blankets to their patrons to use while dining and listening to the music.

In the Harbor

Two area marinas offer restaurants with patio dining. Both casual restaurants allow you to hobnob with boaters and hear tales of their river adventures.

Vinney's on the River
at The Hidden Harbor
388 Ninth Ave. W.
St. Paul Park
651-400-0121
www.thehiddenharbor.com

Mississippi Pub
at River Heights Marina
4455 66th St. E., Inver Grove Heights
651-455-4974
www.mississippipub.com

The River Heights Marina is located near the Rock Island Swing Bridge, which has recently been restored for use as a recreational pier, and the newest paved section of the 27-mile Mississippi River Regional Trail.

Best View

American Legion
50 Sibley St., Hastings
651-437-2046; http://legionpost47.com/
Vibe: casual, old-school

In my opinion, the American Legion has the best view of any of the patios I visited. The food is decent, and the view is stunning. This mid-sized patio overlooks a lovely riverfront park and a view of history-in-the-making. The Legion is in the shadow of the historic blue river bridge, being demolished to make way for the new free-standing arch bridge that is currently under construction. (Bridge opened in November 2013.)

Paddling with a Purpose

July 2013

Those who canoe or kayak do so for many different reasons. I have a handful of my own that justify the tremendous effort it takes to retrieve my kayak from my shed, lash it to my truck and drive it down to the river.

Granted, the effort is caused my own foolishness. My kayak hangs in the back of my shed, directly behind my canoe. They both hover over my instruments of lawn manipulation: mower, weed sprayer, tiller, aerator, etc. I use my kayak more frequently than my canoe so I don't know why I continue to store it in the most hard-to-reach space. I suspect it has to do with tradition. I purchased my kayak many years before my canoe and that's where I've always stored it.

To retrieve it, I must duck under my canoe, climb around the lawn equipment, free it from its chains and try to squeeze it through a narrow opening toward the door. I have to contort my body to accomplish this act and I invariably graze my head against the side of my canoe before the task is done.

This scenario played out for the umpteenth time on June 2, but alas, by 7 p.m. I had reached the river, squeezed myself into my kayak and was gliding along a tranquil surface. The Mississippi can often be rough and choppy but that day it was serene and glassy, and gloriously reflected the bluff line and the ribbons of clouds in the blue sky above.

I embarked from the boat ramp near Spring Lake Park Reserve, located between Rosemount and Hastings. Within minutes I was paddling over the submerged shoreline that separated Spring Lake and the Mississippi river before the Army Corps of Engineers dammed the river and conjoined the two into one body of water. I sprinted across the main channel and paddled around one of several small islands. I like to paddle between these islands because the water is too shallow for motorboats, and the signs of urban progress are hidden from landscape, making me feel like I'm in a wilderness area. I eyed a lovely little cove, pointed my boat in its direction and stroked toward it. Once there, I let myself drift silently along.

I looked like a compass needle trying to find true north as I listened to a beautiful symphony from my feathered friends around me. Minutes later I paddled further along and the water became increasingly more shallow — three feet, two feet, a foot — and very muddy. I was nearly immobile in the muck when six or eight torpedos suddenly burst out from both sides of my bow. I couldn't tell what they were but I heard their report and saw the rippled direction of their trajectory fan out before me to a distance of ten yards or more. They startled me and I sat there in bemusement, feeling like the Sealion submarine that had just fired its load of armament. I stroked further ahead and unexpectedly began to feel several thumps beneath my kayak and see more commotion beneath the surface. I feared that the hunter had become the hunted.

That week, I called Joel Stiras, a fisheries biologist with the Minnesota Department of Natural Resources, to see what caused this underwater barrage. It was likely bigmouth buffalo, he said. The bigmouth buffalo is the largest member of the sucker family and lives in shallow, muddy areas of lakes and rivers. They can grow to three feet or longer and weigh more than 50 pounds.

This experience made me realize why I continue to carve out time to spend on the river. No two outings are ever the same.

Treasure Hunting

August 2013

I was standing in front of the Science Museum of Minnesota squinting into the sun as a young National Park Service ranger fiddled with a hand-held GPS unit, one of several that can be rented free for one week. She quickly pushed some buttons and navigated to a screen that displayed all nine park-sponsored geocache locations in the Mississippi National River and Recreation Area. I watched her demonstration intently since I have never before used a hand-held GPS. It looked simple enough yet I wanted to make sure I understood the most critical piece of equipment required for my first-ever geocache search, which is essentially a high-tech scavenger hunt. I was eager to get on my way so when asked if I wanted to try locating the cache at the MNRRA visitor center, located inside the Science Museum, I declined. Besides, she had already told me that this particular GPS unit doesn't work well indoors, and she also let slip the location of the cache.

Geocaching has been growing in popularity since it was introduced in May 2000. The sport is simple: punch a coordinate into a GPS, travel to the general vicinity of the location and start searching for the geocache. A man named Matt Stum is credited with coining that term. The prefix "geo" refers to the earth and "cache" is a French term for a hiding place. A geocache is typically a small plastic container hidden outdoors that contains a logbook and often a small trinket. The general rule is that if you take the trinket you leave something in its place.

To start my adventure, I looped the GPS lanyard around my neck and descended the long flight of steps outside the Science Museum that led toward Shepard Road and the Mississippi River. My coordinate was GC20CGC, entitled Grain Movers. I deduced that the cache must be hidden near the St. Paul Grain Terminal at the Upper Landing, so I headed west toward it on the Sam Morgan Trail.

I watched as the distance to my goal on the GPS clicked lower and lower: 50 feet, 30 feet, finally 10 feet. At this point I stopped and held the unit squarely in front of me, as the ranger had instructed. I felt rather odd as I spun around trying to get the GPS to signal with a beep that I'd arrived. I got within 7 feet, but heard no beep. I let the unit fall to my chest and began searching. There is not much at that spot to look under, so I searched in vain for several minutes. I wondered if the cache was inside the grain terminal so I rattled the door. Locked.

I thought about searching for another nearby cache hidden along the riverbank only a few hundred yards away but decided against it because the ranger told me that particular cache hasn't been found in over a year. I suspect the river swallowed it up last spring and it's now somewhere in Mississippi or Louisiana. I felt defeated, yet challenged. I checked the GPS for another nearby cache. It registered one near Fort Snelling so I retraced my steps back to my car and headed for the historic site. As I got near, I glanced at the GPS to see if I was close. I was. I was also reminded of a "distracted driving" presentation I'd seen the day before so I took my eyes off the unit, focused on the road and steered toward the fort. I didn't want to get a ticket for driving while geocaching.

From the parking lot, I walked down the paved trail toward the fort, which was teeming with tourists. From the fort, the trail veered south and quickly led me to my destination. It was a grassy area with huge sandstone slabs that provided a perfect resting place for weary hikers or a small group of picnickers. Nearby was a large cottonwood tree. I rustled through the tall grass and circled the tree looking for the cache, to no avail. I walked to the stone slabs and searched around them as well. At one point my GPS registered me at zero feet. Still I found nothing. I looked over at the fort and saw a large group enter. Rather than admitting defeat once again, I reasoned that the cache must have been stolen. I imagined a deviant freckled-faced fourth grader finding it on a field trip and slyly slipping it into his backpack.

I walked back to the parking lot, but before going to my car I meandered over to a scenic overlook. I found myself disenchanted with the sport until I gazed at the panoramic view of the river valley, illuminated by the warm sun that shone brightly from a cloudless blue sky, and at the river, which was brown and foamy and running fast from a month of rain. I was happy to be there and happy that I'd spent the last two hours tromping around the river valley. At that moment, I understood what J. R. R. Tolkien meant when he wrote, "Not all who wander are lost."

I Wonder as I Wander

September 2013

Two trails converged in a yellow wood. At least that's what Dakota County Parks hopes will happen in the coming year with a yet-to-be-developed 3.8-mile segment of the Mississippi River Trail in Dakota County. The undeveloped section prohibits cyclists from safely cruising from South St. Paul to Hastings along the riverfront unencumbered by vehicle traffic.

The trail is paved to where it meets the gap. The portion north from Hastings was completed last year and the route running from South St. Paul was paved this year. The gap remains in the Pine Bend area in Rosemount and Nininger Township.

Dakota County Parks, which is spearheading the 27-mile project, is in the process of finalizing the trail alignment through the Nininger area. A route was selected in late May and surveying work has begun, with construction to start next summer. The County also plans to initiate a feasibility study later this year to find a suitable trail alignment around the Union Pacific railroad tracks in Rosemount.

I traveled to this area recently to view the project site. Pine Bend Trail intersects Highway 55 just east of Highway 52 and winds through an industrial area to where it crosses the tracks. At this point it becomes gravel and darts straightaway toward Lower Spring Lake Park Reserve, a beautiful nature sanctuary filled with native prairie grasses, flowers and old-growth woods, as well as an archery range and youth camp and lodge. Traveling a half-mile farther and turning left onto Fischer Avenue, one can see where land has been cleared to survey the trail. Fischer leads to a gravel cul-de-sac by the river, and it is near here that the Minnesota Department of Natural Resources hopes to build a new recreation area and boat ramp, which would be easily accessible by trail users. Although that project will not likely begin for a few years, I wanted to see this site because of its historical significance. It's the former location of Bud's Landing, a small resort that catered to hunters and fishermen for half a century.

A sign forbidding trespassing stands near a metal

gate that blocks access to a narrow road that winds down to the river and the former resort. I ducked under the gate and started down the pathway, which was rutted and overgrown with vegetation. This land, now owned by Dakota County, once belonged to the Josephs family. The late Bud Josephs, who lived on St. Paul's West Side and made his living as a meat cutter at Swift in South St. Paul, purchased the land in three separate transactions between 1943 and 1947 and transformed it into Bud's Hunting and Fishing Resort. In the spring of 2012, the Josephs family sold the land to the county with the condition that the area be preserved as Bud's Landing.

Even though I was on public land, the "No Trespassing" sign made me uneasy as I ambled down the path. As the forest opened to the riverbank I could see what was left of the former resort. At one time there were three cabins on the property. All that remains are one cabin and a building that housed a rustic bar. It's a place that time has quietly stepped around.

A large, grassy area abuts the boat landing, which is now stuffed with whitened logs that have floated down the river and become lodged in the gentle bend of the riverbank. With a little work, the site will make a nice area for future generations to enjoy and gain access to the river. It's a beautiful area that is worthy of preserving and enhancing.

I walked around the bar and the cabin, both of which are in a serious state of disrepair. I peered into the windows and tried to imagine what the buildings were like when they were filled with laughter and braggadocio from resort patrons. I envisioned grown men huddled around the bar, dressed in flannel, with stubble on their chins and greasy hair matted against their scalps from being tucked under a hat all day. With a Grain Belt beer in hand and a Lucky Strike cigarette dangling from his lips and bouncing as he talked, one would be telling a story in the smoky haze about the big one that got away, or ribbing his mate about the easy shot that he missed when the first mallards of the day came circling in over the misty waters of a crisp autumn dawn.

It's evident that these buildings were never luxurious or pretentious. They weren't meant to be. They were built for people who love the outdoors and who enjoy a rustic setting to relax in after a full day on the river. It's intriguing to me how structures like these can be neglected to the point of no return, but I know that it stems from the tidal wave of "progress" and people's desire to have something new, something better. Oftentimes, as property is handed down from one generation to the next, there comes a point when it's no longer feasible for the heirs to maintain the property. Sometimes it's due to finances, other times to proximity and not being able to visit the property often enough to maintain it. Slowly, year after year, nature beats at buildings like these and tries to reclaim the land beneath them. Today, the wood siding and roofs on both structures are rotted and pocked with holes that freely let in the elements.

At the back of the cabin, lying in tall grass next to several rusted 55-gallon oil drums, is the faceplate of an old jukebox. I bent down and looked at the songs listed on it. One was the 1964 hit, "Those Wonderful Years" by Webb Price. Suddenly, I heard a quarter enter a thin metal slot and clunk below. A motor whirred and lifted a vinyl disk into position. The needle popped down on the record and melancholy music filled the air.

Undoubtedly those were wonderful years.

Running with the Goats

October 2013

On Friday, Aug. 30, Keith Hill and Lynette Nadeau drove their pickup truck to the backcountry of Flint Hills Resources' Pine Bend refinery property in Rosemount. Hitched to the truck was an 8-by-16-foot trailer with wooden sides, covered by a tattered canvas tarp. Inside were 80 Savanna and Spanish goats, stomping their hooves, bleating and jostling for position to be the first to escape their confinement.

Hill opened the narrow gate on the back of the trailer and the goats charged out wildly and sprinted toward an all-you-can-eat buffet. For two weeks, these goats and about 50 others would graze five acres of fenced property along the Mississippi River in an area known as the Pine Bend Bluffs Natural Area.

The goats are part of an innovative approach to restoring natural habitat along the river. Footing the bill for the project is St. Paul-based Great River Greening (GRG), a nonprofit that works on conservation projects on both public and private land. Since 1995, GRG has enlisted the help of more than 30,000 volunteers to remove exotic species, to plant native trees, shrubs, wildflowers and grasses, and assist with other projects. A common—and tedious—project for GRG volunteers is the removal of buckthorn. There's nothing complicated about that process. Volunteers simply venture into a section of woods infested with the plant, yank it from the ground or cut it with a hand tool and drag it away.

For the past seven years Hill and Nadeau, owners of Goat Peak Ranch in Red Wing, have been using their goats to control buckthorn and other noxious weeds. According to Hill, goats are not picky about their meals and will eat just about anything put before them: grass, shrubs, bushes, small trees, maybe even your shoe. They particularly enjoy the leafy buckthorn and will chomp it down to the ground.

Wiley Buck, restoration ecologist with Great River Greening, was there when the goats were released. He touted the grazing practice for its efficiency. He said goats do the tough work of removing buckthorn and other underbrush so natural habitat can grow in its place. He also said that fewer chemicals are needed to treat an area that has been grazed. Also, as goats move from shrub to shrub, their hooves imbed native seeds into the ground to help restore the natural prairie and oak savanna woodland, which is important habitat for millions of songbirds, waterfowl and shorebirds that use the Mississippi River flyway migration corridor. Flint Hills has worked with GRG and Friends of the Mississippi River, another St. Paul-based environmental nonprofit, since 2000 to restore the Pine Bend Bluffs Natural Area.

I wanted to see the goats in action so I followed them into the woods. While goats aren't finicky about what they eat, it appears they don't like to be watched while they eat because they quickly scooted off to the far end of the 5-acre site. I tried to walk quietly through the woods to sneak up on them, but as I trudged through the underbrush I made a racket as I pulled through vines, snapped twigs and climbed over downed trees.

Finally, I found the goats. The agile creatures were huddled on the side of a steep ravine, dutifully doing their job. It was amusing to watch them eat. Occasionally, one would look at me—his soft floppy ears darting out from under his curved horns, his beard tickling the foliage beneath him—and then move away. Inevitably, the rest of the herd slowly followed.

I looked at the forest and realized how much work they had to do. They were on the clock but didn't appear to mind the massive job before them. I guess if you're a goat, it's good work, if you can get it.

War and Peace

November 2013

In reflecting upon my travels throughout the Mississippi National River and Recreation Area this past year, I realized that I have spent considerably more time in the central and southern area of the corridor than the northern end. Before this year-long series comes to an end, I wanted to fully explore the northern reaches. On my to-do list was paddling near the confluence of the Crow River, visiting the Banfill-Locke Center for the Arts and hiking within the Islands of Peace Recreation Area. These areas are significant because the confluence of the Crow marks the northern boundary of the park, and here the Mississippi is designated as a Minnesota Wild and Scenic River. The Banfill-Locke Center for the Arts is listed on the National Register of Historic Sites, and Islands of Peace Park is important for what it promotes.

One Saturday morning I drove to a boat launch on the edge of the small town of Dayton to start my paddle. The September morn was clear and calm and I was pleased to have the river to myself. From studying my map, I knew this section has rapids but I wasn't prepared for how quickly I would be upon them. The rapids, which are little more than a riffle, are only about a hundred yards from the launch but stretch across nearly the entire breadth of the river. They were challenging not for their swiftness but because of the low level of water that ran through them. Before I could properly scout my path, my kayak was scratching the rocky bottom, and then I became stuck. On shore residents of Dayton were crowded in a city park celebrating their fall festival. I suddenly felt like I was part of their entertainment. I could hear their snickers of laughter and feel their judgmental stares and as I struggled to push myself along to find enough water to float through. I desperately hoped I wouldn't have to get out and drag my boat over the rocks. Eventually I found deeper water and quickly paddled out of sight.

Downstream I didn't fare much better. I tried to paddle around an island but again was thwarted by low, impassable water. After learning my lesson, I stayed in the deep, main channel for the remainder of my outing. As I paddled back to the launch, I was apprehensive about returning through the rapids and past the crowd. Fortunately, I found deep water on the opposing bank and expertly maneuvered around the rapids. I could hear cheers and applause from the park. I imagined it was for me but knew better.

As I exited the parking lot I was surprised to see a large number of people lining the street. They were scurrying to set up lawn chairs for what I presumed was a parade. A small gaggle of wide-eyed elementary school girls jumped up and down excitedly when they saw my blue kayak perched high on top of my truck. I believe they thought I was the first entrant in the parade. I drove slowly through town and expected a sour-faced traffic cop to glare at me and wave me off the street, but none appeared. I imagined the pop of a public announcement system coming to life and an enthusiastic voice greeting the crowd: "And our first unit in this year's parade is the fool who got his kayak stuck in the middle of the river." The crowd cheered. I waved to them and tossed out Tootsie Rolls and other assorted candies.

Before visiting Islands of Peace, I made a brief stop at the Banfill-Locke Center for the Arts, located in Fridley near where Rice Creek enters the Mississippi. This historic Greek revival structure once served as a tavern and inn. John Banfill built it in 1847 to serve soldiers, fur traders and other travelers along the Red River Trail. After the property changed hands several times, the Locke family purchased it in 1912 and used it as a dairy farm. After closing that operation, they made it their summer home.

Today, the building serves as a community arts center. I went inside and viewed a display of abstract art in the gallery, my footsteps echoing loudly as I moved across the wooden floor from one piece of art to the next. The art was interesting but it wasn't nearly as impressive to me as were the thoughts of how many travelers have passed through these halls before me, and of the many families that have gathered in these rooms for special occasions and for everyday living. I walked up a creaky staircase and peeked into a room where a group of painters was quietly putting brush to canvas. It's good to see that this historic structure has been preserved for the community.

Islands of Peace Park is not far from the Banfill-Locke Center. It's a scenic sanctuary of three islands: Chase, Durnham and Gil Hodges. Chase is the only one accessible by a pedestrian bridge. Two structures near the trailhead commemorate the park's homage to peace. The first is a granite memorial surrounded by flags, dedicated by American Legion Shaddrick LaBeau Post 303 as "A tribute to the men and women who served America in times of war and peace." The other is a wooden sign bearing a quote from Edward T. Wilmes, who founded the park in 1971. It says, "Islands of Peace: Where Peace Is A Way of Life Every Hour of Every Day for All Those Willing to Share the Experience."

The words were encouraging. As of late, I've been

too focused on personal issues, the fractures in our country, and the ever looming threat of more military intervention around the world. I, like many, come to the river seeking answers, seeking peace, and this park was an appropriate place to do just that.

I ventured into the park and walked out to Chase Island to "share the experience." There is nothing on the tranquil island except three benches and a paved trail that weaves through mature maple and basswood trees. On the southern end of the island is a wide beach filled with soft sand and smooth stones. It more resembles a beach on Lake Superior's North Shore than the muddy, grassy beaches so common on the Mississippi. I walked down to the water and was amazed at how clear it was. I've never seen the river this clear anywhere else. Evidently the gracious amounts of sand and stone have filtered it clean.

The river beckoned me to come closer so I kicked off my shoes, peeled off my socks and waded in, its cool water soothing my feet. I looked to my left and saw the I-694 bridge, with its steady stream of traffic and never-ending din. I wished it weren't there disturbing my peace, but like the unrest in this world, I knew I had to accept it. I turned around and looked upstream. Nothing man-made was visible, just the green riverbank and the gentle rolling river flowing around the islands. I was happy I had turned around. That simple act changed my perspective and allowed me to see the beauty around me. And find peace.

Holidays on the Hill

December 2013

Gently falling snow teased by a cool northerly breeze enhances the nostalgic charm of St. Paul's Summit Avenue unlike any other time of the year. In the dim light of December, one can envision horses clomping along the avenue pulling carriages filled with the well-dressed and well-mannered men and women of the Gilded Age. Among the best known of that era is James J. Hill, who built his brooding castle on the avenue and lived there until his death on May 29, 1916. At that time he was one of the wealthiest people in America, with a personal fortune valued at $63 million.

Today, his house is a popular tourist destination for those interested in that industrious era, a time when some men got rich beyond their wildest dreams. The Hill House offers holiday tours to provide a glimpse of the home and the family who lived there. The tours are led by costumed actors who use a script based on letters and oral histories of people who worked for the Hill family. I toured the home this fall before staff started decorating the house with pink and yellow ribbons and pink roses. It's an unconventional choice for holiday decorations, but Mrs. Hill preferred that combination over the traditional red and green.

As I toured the mansion, one word came to mind: ostentatious. It's really the only word that can aptly describe the Hill House, which sits on a lovely 3-acre estate overlooking the Mississippi River. When Hill, his wife Mary and eight of their 10 children moved there in 1891 (one child died in infancy and the eldest was married by the time the home was built), the home was the largest and most luxurious residence in the state. It was then and still is today an impressive architectural wonder.

How big is it? It's big. The 36,000-square-foot, 5-story home has 20 bedrooms, 13 bathrooms and 22 fireplaces. That's 3,600 square feet per inhabitant, and one bathroom each. No waiting in line for the Hill family. Even with the dozen or so servants who lived there, that's still a lot of elbow room per person.

They didn't scrimp on the fineries either, inside or out. Stained glass windows, crystal chandeliers, inlaid marble floors and elaborately carved oak and mahogany woodwork bear testament to that. The home also features mechanical systems that were extremely sophisticated for the day, including central heating, indoor plumbing with hot and cold running water, gas and electric lighting and an advanced ventilation system that circulated air throughout the home.

But wait, there's more. The house has a 100-foot reception hall, a 2-story gallery for Hill's significant art collection, a room with a stage and seating for 200, and a dining room that features a walk-in safe accessible only through a hidden door.

How did they keep the kids entertained? They played them tunes on the grand piano or the 1,006-pipe organ, or they shooed them to the fourth floor to play on the gymnastic equipment.

Hill was 53 when he moved in and he lived there for a quarter-century. He spent the first 20 years of his career amassing wealth by working in shipping on the Mississippi and Red rivers. His first business, James J. Hill and Co., was headquartered near the Lower Landing in Lowertown. He turned his efforts toward rail and eventually pushed his Great Northern Railway from St. Paul westward across North Dakota, Montana and Washington to the Pacific Ocean, opening the Upper Midwest and Pacific Northwest to development. His railway, which transported timber, coal, wheat and copper, is the predecessor to the BNSF railway that runs along the Mississippi through the Twin Cities today.

Hill was known as a shrewd businessman with a short temper. It's perplexing to think of all the luxuries in his home, and then learn that he was not there often to enjoy them, as he frequently traveled across the country and abroad tending to his many business affairs. Quite simply, he was a workaholic. Before he died, a newspaper reporter asked him for the secret of his success and he replied, "Work, hard work, intelligent work, and then more work."

Hill's bedroom has a large window that overlooks the Mississippi River. It offers a wonderful, panoramic view of the river valley, but we don't know if he appreciated it. Did he wake up each morning and gaze upon the river or simply walk by the window with his mind clogged with other things? Even though he was involved in early conservation efforts, we have no records of whether or not he saw beauty in the land that he lived on, and in the land he helped open to others.

There is a wealth of information gleaned from diaries and personal papers about his business dealings but little is known of his personal life. What we do know, according to Hill House site manager Craig Johnson, who wrote the holiday tour script, is that Hill was usually home for the holidays but he often got sick during that time, presumably from being overworked. He enjoyed playing games with his large number of grandchildren and showing them his prized paintings.

Now featured in the art gallery is a wonderful collection of historic paintings entitled Minnesota Waters. The display allows you to see what the Mississippi River looked like in Hill's day. Paintings include depictions of the river in St. Paul, Fort Snelling and St. Anthony Falls, including one winter landscape showing Hill's famous Stone Arch Bridge.

Hill had a large library in his home with floor-to-ceiling cases containing many volumes of books. I wonder if he owned a copy of "A Christmas Carol," written by Charles Dickens, a popular author of Hill's day. I hope Hill was visited by a few Christmas ghosts of his own so he was able to enjoy his holidays on the hill and understand that a man's true legacy extends far beyond his wealth and power.

Riding the Rails through the River Valley

February 2014

Just before noon a taxi pulled up in front of Amtrak's Midway station in St. Paul. A middle-aged couple got out, retrieved their luggage and entered the station, joining the several dozen other passengers who had gathered there for Train #8, providing service to Chicago and points in between. Some of the passengers had been there for several hours because the train was scheduled to depart at 7:50 a.m. Others filtered in much later, including me. I arrived at 11:30 a.m., knowing the train was delayed by four hours. This was my first time riding Amtrak and my experience proved to be both challenging and rewarding.

Sometime in March Amtrak will shutter its Midway station and begin offering service at Union Depot in downtown St. Paul. For 36 years, rail passengers have passed through the Midway hub while traveling the Empire Builder route, which connects the Twin Cities to Chicago and Seattle. I wanted to be among those numbers before the relocation occurred so I decided to take a quick jaunt from St. Paul to Red Wing, the first stop on the eastbound route, about an hour away.

I purchased a ticket for $12 online on the last Thursday in January to travel the following day. That evening I received a text message informing me that the train was delayed by weather and was expected to be 10 hours late. I called the customer service line and was told I had two options. I could receive a refund or they would bus me to Red Wing. I took the refund.

The same scenario played out the following week. I booked a ticket, was notified of a 12-hour delay and opted for the refund. The Empire Builder route has been plagued with long delays in recent months, caused by both the weather and the high number of crude oil shipments coming out of North Dakota. Amtrak shares the tracks with freight trains, which always receive top priority. Undeterred, I booked another ticket the following week. An incredulous laugh escaped me as I checked my phone that evening and read a text message announcing a four-hour delay. Fortunately, I could adjust my schedule to accommodate that time frame and my trip was on.

The Midway station is in a rather desolate industrial area, which doesn't provide a favorable impression of the city to first-time visitors. Once inside, it was quickly evident that Amtrak already had its sights set on Union Depot. The brown tile floor inside the doorway looked like it hadn't been mopped in a week and the carpeting in the waiting area was soiled. Granted, it's difficult to keep flooring clean during the wintertime, but the waiting area was cold, the walls were marred and the bathrooms unkempt, making me think the company had already given up on the place. Even the snack machine was neglected. A handwritten sign taped to it read: "Out of Order, Again."

About 50 people filled the waiting area. They were a somber bunch, yet none were visibly impatient with the delay. I suspect they were veteran rail travelers who expected scheduling conflicts. They simply chatted with each other or buried their noses either in books or electronic devices.

Just after noon, a man picked up a microphone and informed us that the train had arrived, and then issued boarding instructions. Amtrak staff were friendly and courteous as they quickly boarded us and got us on our way.

I was pleasantly surprised at the size and comfort of the seats, which are arranged in rows of two on each side of the train. They are wide and have a generous amount of leg room, allowing even a long-legged person to comfortably stretch out.

The train departed smoothly and silently, and it wasn't long before we were traveling through tree-filled neighborhoods along the Mississippi River. The scenery improves as the train rounds a bend and turns toward downtown St. Paul. To our right is Harriet Island, with its open spaces, historic stone pavilion, and floating entertainment venues. To our left is the downtown skyline. We pass by Union Depot and I see the long brick concourse reaching out toward the river. This renovated landmark, with its marble floors, spacious waiting room and windows overlooking the river, will provide a wonderful first impression for first-time visitors. Furthermore, those experiencing long delays will be able to meander into the city for a cup of coffee, a meal at a nearby restaurant or shopping, something that is impossible to do at the Midway station.

As the train lumbers away from downtown the landscape begins to change and we pass beneath large sandstone bluffs. A passenger in front of me nudges her companion and points out the window to a hawk surfing an airstream overhead. It is suspended high above us, moving only slightly side to side, not forward or backward. We all marvel at the sight.

We stop briefly next to a freight train and I examine its cars, some of which are splashed with colorful graffiti. I am taken back to my youth and the time I first rode the rails. It was a warm summer evening and my friends and I heard the wail of the train whistle as it approached the center of our small town. We huddled together, devised a plan and then ran to the tracks and hopped into an open box car and rode it to the edge of town. As the train started to gain speed, we jumped out and walked back to town along the tracks. This became an impromptu activity for a short period of time. We eventually got braver and climbed to the top of the railroad cars and jumped between them as the train rolled along.

The freight train next to us lunged forward and its thunder-like rumble jolted me back to the present. I shrugged off the foolishness of my youthful adventures, retrieved my coat, and headed to the dining car, where I ordered a cup of coffee and took a seat. The dining car is a cheery place with numerous windows, skylights and comfortable sofa-style seating that faces outward. Jazz played softly in the background as I settled in to enjoy the view.

Once we passed under I-494 the scenery quickly turned rural, and quaint hobby farms and fields dotted the countryside. Next we rolled past the Grey Cloud Dunes Scientific and Natural Area near Cottage Grove and I saw a deer make its way across a gentle slope high above the river. Before long we were at the river's edge, traveling so close to it that I couldn't see the shoreline below me. At this point, the metro area feels far away. We passed Grey Cloud Island and the steamy confluence of a creek—or more likely a drainage pipe—where ducks and geese were playing in the small pool of water. Next we passed Lock and Dam #2 at Hastings, where large sheets of ice were scattered below the dam, looking like a window had fallen from heaven and shattered into a thousand pieces. At Hastings, we crossed a trestle and were treated to spectacular views of the river, the new Highway 61 Bridge that opened last summer and the historic downtown district filled with 2- and 3-story brick buildings and the old courthouse, with its dome dominating the skyline.

South of Hastings, civilization disappears and we rumbled through the flood plain and the Vermillion River bottoms. Tall marsh grasses and trees that thrive in swampy water dominated the snow-covered landscape, and the tracks of deer, fox and rabbits made mosaic patterns in the snow, always zig-zagging to the right and left, around a tree, under a fallen branch. We passed by cornfields and working farms with boxy barns and skinny silos, a small cemetery and a 100-acre marsh with tall amber grasses swaying in the wind, looking like a sea of ripened wheat.

I could tell we'd gained speed. Now the train was rapidly cruising along, rhythmically rocking back and forth. We zipped past Treasure Island Casino and the adjacent Prairie Island Indian community, and the Xcel Energy nuclear plant, all of which seem to be located in the middle of nowhere. At last we neared Red Wing, where big bluff country begins. We continued along the river, past a marina and into the charming downtown district. The train stopped and I reluctantly got off. I wish I could have continued on for another two hours to La Crosse, where the train leaves the river and darts east across Wisconsin, but my wife was waiting to take me back to St. Paul, back to my deadlines and back to my business that, unlike Amtrak, runs on a fairly rigid and predictable schedule. The change of pace had been refreshing.

In the Footsteps of the Faithful

March 2014

It's a grey March afternoon and I am standing on the riverbank in Harriet Island Regional Park gazing up at the Cathedral of Saint Paul, which is perched majestically on one of St. Paul's fabled seven hills. With its 120-foot-wide copper dome rising more than 300 feet into the air, it's an imposing and impressive structure that dominates a gap in the city's western skyline. The sight and sound of movement is all around me, intrusive noises caused by traffic, sirens, machinery. But amidst it all, I hear something special coming from the Cathedral: the peal of the bells. Deep, rich tones emanate from the bell tower, riding the breeze toward me and reverberating throughout the river valley. It's a comforting sound that reminds all who hear it to pause and reflect.

Church bells have been used since the first century to remind the faithful to take time from their busy day to stop and pray, and to announce the beginning of a service. Historically, bells were rung at 6 a.m., noon and 6 p.m., beckoning people to recite the Lord's Prayer. The Cathedral of Saint Paul rings its bells every quarter hour from 7 a.m. to 6 p.m. weekdays, and until 8 p.m. on Saturdays. Longer peals happen at noon and 6 p.m., and on Sundays before each Mass.

The sound has me thinking of the people who followed a call to this area, and the impact they made on this community. It started with Father Lucien Galtier, who came to the hardscrabble village of Pig's Eye in 1840 to minister to French Canadians who were living there at the time. In 1841, he built a small log chapel on the bluff in what is today Kellogg Park near Robert and Kellogg, and dedicated it to the Apostle Paul. He quickly petitioned for the village to be renamed for the patron saint as well. Over a period of 74 years, his burgeoning congregation moved three times before finally building the present-day Cathedral. Archbishop John Ireland celebrated the first Mass there on March 28, 1915, Palm Sunday.

The Catholic community in St. Paul is renowned for its social outreach, especially the Dorothy Day Center that is operated by Catholic Charities. The center provides hot meals, temporary housing, mental health services and medical care to several thousands of homeless people each year.

Not far behind Father Galtier was Harriet Bishop, who traveled to St. Paul on the Mississippi River by steamboat. She arrived in 1847 to start the first school and Sunday School. That Sunday School evolved into a congregation—the First Baptist Church of St. Paul—that is still active today. Its social ministries include providing temporary shelter for families in need, resettlement housing and transportation services to refugees from Burma who are living in St. Paul, and a variety of projects with other organizations, including the Dorothy Day Center, Naomi Family Center, Martha's Closet, Listening House and SafeZone.

One of the city's most notable early African Americans was the Rev. Robert Hickman, a slave from Missouri who helped a group of people in that state escape slavery in 1863. The band of believers traveled upriver on a raft. Along the harrowing journey, they were spotted by a benevolent steamboat captain, who towed them to St. Paul. Shortly after arriving, they formed the Pilgrim Baptist Church, which is still active today. The congregation commemorated their inaugural service with a baptismal service on the shores of the Mississippi River.

The Jewish community has made its mark on people in the city as well. In 1897, the women of Mount Zion Temple founded a settlement house on the West Side—the Neighborhood House—to assist Russian

Jewish immigrants. Today, the synagogue continues to assist Neighborhood House in offering social services to immigrants, refugees and low-income people, including a food shelf that serves hundreds of people each day.

I look at the river, still encased in ice, and am reminded of the Native Americans who lived on and cared for this land for many centuries. About four miles upstream is Pike Island, located at the confluence of the Mississippi and Minnesota rivers. This is a sacred site and burial ground for the Mendota Mdewakanton Dakota.

I turn around to return to my car and see a large cottonwood tree along the trail with a deep crevice in it. I can see writing within the 6-inch-wide fissure so I step closer to get a better look. Enscribed in thick black ink are the words "Lord Jesus Saves." It appears the faithful are still making their mark along the river in more ways than one.

Three Days. Two Friends. One Canoe.

A trip through the Mississippi National River and Recreation Area

The morning of September 4 broke to gray skies filled with fine mist. It wasn't much precipitation, just enough to keep me fiddling with the windshield wipers every few minutes as we drove through the remnants of rush hour traffic on our way to a boat ramp in Dayton, Minn., where my friend Tharren and I would embark on a 3-day canoe trip through the Mississippi National River and Recreation Area. This trip has been a dream of mine for several years but has eluded me until this point.

My wife Jil was with us—she would drive the van home, an hour away, giving us no way to get to our destination except by paddling—and she joined Tharren in peppering me with questions to see if I had thoroughly considered the logistics of our trip:

"How far are we going the first day?"

"Twenty-five miles, from Dayton to downtown Minneapolis."

"Where will you keep the canoe?"

"We're going to stash it in the brush along the riverbank."

Eyebrows were raised and I was accused of being foolhardy.

"They do that?" asked Tharren.

"I'm not sure if *they* do," I said. "But *we* are. I scouted out an area last weekend."

Jil was sure someone would steal the canoe and our trip would be over before we were even half-way done and she cautioned me against leaving it along the river.

Their questions made me uneasy, although I didn't admit it to them. I've been on many other paddling trips but they've always been to the backcountry. I've never taken an extended trip through an urban area, where we would face not only the elements, but also have to navigate around the turbulent wakes of barges and yachts and around dams and through locks, not to mention the increased chances of someone stealing our canoe or gear while we were off sleeping or exploring an interesting area.

We pushed off at 9:30 a.m. at river mile 879, which means we were 879 miles from the beginning of the Lower Mississippi River, near Cairo, Ill. By now it was 74 degrees and the rain had mostly subsided. Tharren was in the bow and I in the stern. It would remain this way the entire trip because he has very little paddling experience. I could sense his uneasiness and chuckled to myself because I knew what he was thinking. My intuition stems from knowing him for nearly 35 years. We met in the eighth grade, an awkward time in our lives when our testosterone was pumping wildly and we could think about little else than dating girls and making the varsity wrestling team as freshmen. Now we're in the shadow of 50—trying to ignore the wrinkles forming around our eyes and our expanding waistlines—and we think about matters much deeper and closer to the heart.

Through it all, we've shared a love for nature and outdoor adventure. It started with a camping trip shortly after I got my driver's license. It began poorly when our map got sucked out the window of my blue hatchback Pinto as we sped down the freeway on our way to a state park. We camped in a mostly waterproof orange nylon pup tent and lost our food the first night to hungry raccoons. We've learned from our mistakes and for the past 20 years have carved out time each year for a new adventure. Many of our trips have included scaling rugged peaks in the Rocky Mountains and the Tetons, and backpacking hikes through some of the country's most beautiful national parks.

The Mississippi River near Dayton is designated as a Minnesota Wild and Scenic River. I kayaked this area last fall during low water and got stuck briefly on the rocks of the small rapids located about 100 yards from the boat ramp. This year the river is high and swift and we were quickly swept along in the fast-moving current, which made paddling easy and enjoyable.

Much of the shoreline here is lined with houses visible from the river, ranging from small ramblers to small mansions. In some stretches, seemingly every home had a dock with a pontoon boat tied to it. At mile 876, just three miles from where we started, the riverfront transformed into thick, lush hardwood forest as we traveled between Foster and Cloquet islands, bordered by Mississippi West Regional Park. About six miles farther the river widened and the approaching wind whipped the water into 2-foot high waves. A rogue 3-foot breaker crashed into us and left some of the river in the bottom of our canoe. We paddled hard for nearly two miles until we reached the Coon Rapids Dam, located in the middle of the scenic 160-acre Coon Rapids Dam Regional Park. We pulled off at a boat ramp and portaged around the dam.

With 18 miles behind us, we approached the I-694 Bridge, which buzzed with traffic. We both looked up and marveled at the dichotomy of our surroundings. When Tharren said, "I'm glad I'm not up there," I knew he was beginning to understand why the Mississippi National River and Recreation Area is such a special place. We made a slight turn and suddenly the Minneapolis skyline appeared directly before us, looking as if it were floating in the middle of the river. We paddled along and soon saw the effects of urbanization—more bridges and more industry, the most invasive being the EMR metal recycling plant. We floated slowly by the factory and watched the apocalyptic sight of an excavator digging its powerful clawed arm into a mountain of scrap metal. It lifted some up and dropped it repeatedly to loosen it, causing a roar of thunder, before grabbing a load and depositing it for removal. This is the only area where we could smell the stench of industry, and it smelled toxic. It also affected the way we viewed the river.

"I was thinking about where we've been and what it's like now closer to the city," said Tharren. He paused. "It's kind of sad."

We paddled along and watched as the skyline became framed beneath the Broadway Avenue Bridge, the 8th Avenue Bridge and the Hennepin Avenue Bridge. We had traveled nearly 25 miles and were tired. We paddled to the river's edge, dragged the canoe into the thick brush and picked our way up the riverbank to a railing near a paved trail. Just as Tharren was jumping over the railing a young female runner came by. She gasped when she saw him, grabbed her startled heart and sped on, fueled by adrenaline. We talked about her perceived creepy encounter as we walked two blocks to our hotel, our gear slung over our shoulders in waterproof bags and our muddy shoes leaving footprints from where we stashed the canoe.

Back on the Water

Around 9 a.m. on Friday we warily approached the 800-foot passageway leading to the Upper St. Anthony Falls Lock and searched for instructions to reach the lock operator. We were surrounded by concrete, making us feel like ants on a leaf floating along a curb in a rainstorm. Above us the curved arches of the Central Avenue Bridge bounded gracefully over the river, their bony ribs barely visible in the dark underside shadows. One of the bridge's thick piers on our port side was under attack from a crew of construction workers. They paid no attention to us as they noisily chipped away at its decay with powerful jackhammers, shooting stuttering echoes down the river. Four white stripes on the guide wall fanned out in the distance, following the gentle bend in the river until they appeared to merge into one line, pointing us in the direction of the unknown.

Neither of us spoke but we were both thinking about the scene from the night before when we leaned over the railing of the nearby historic Stone Arch Bridge and peered down at the 400-foot-long lock.

"They do that?" asked Tharren in astonishment, wondering if canoeists were able to lock-through.

"They do," I assured him as we surveyed our surroundings.

The lock is nestled along the west bank, adjacent to a dam that spans the river. Water flows smoothly over the dam but tumbles into a violent, frothy potion below. The sight and sound of the turbulence reveals a small glimpse of what the river once looked like here when it dropped sharply over a 20-foot precipice and careened around jagged limestone slabs below. The falls provided the energy needed to turn the many grain and timber mills that transformed the tiny village of St. Anthony into the industrial powerhouse of Minneapolis.

The signal light near the lock was red, warning us not to approach, so we bobbed on the current near a 2-foot gap in the guide wall that housed a cord. Printed instructions told us to pull the cord to reach the lock operator so Tharren reached out and gave it a yank.

"Yes?" a voice squealed from a speaker above.

"We want to lock through," we shouted in unison, hoping to be heard over the roar of jackhammers.

There was a short pause. "Are you in a canoe?"

"Yes," we said, still speaking in tandem. I assumed he looked our way from the lock house but was unable to see us.

"OK. It will be about fifteen minutes to get the chamber ready."

We waited patiently and started paddling once the signal light burned green.

Inside, we watched the doors close slowly behind us, trapping us in the 56- by 400-foot liquid elevator. A lock worker appeared above us, greeted us warmly and offered much-appreciated advice.

"How far will we drop?" I asked.

"About fifty feet," he said. "Just hang on to the floating buoy." He turned to walk away. "I'll let the lower lock know you're coming."

Tharren was closest to the metal cylinder so he grabbed hold of the rope attached to it. Before long, we began to slowly sink until finally the dark, wet, concrete walls towered 49 feet above us. A horn blew, telling us it was time to leave, so we dipped our paddles and headed toward the St. Anthony Lower Lock, about a half-mile downstream.

The swirling eddies just outside the lock made paddling challenging and I noticed Tharren wasn't putting in his usual effort.

"We need to dig hard to get through this," I commanded.

"Shut up," he snapped. "I'm scared."

I smiled. *Good*, I thought to myself. Every adventure should include a degree of fear. Actually, I was relishing the shoe being on the other foot. On past trips while climbing mountain walls with precipitous drops I was normally the one trembling.

We felt fortunate to go through the lock because it is scheduled to close on or before June 10, 2015. While details of its future are uncertain, the U.S. Army Corps of Engineers says the closure is being done to help stop the movement of Asian carp, an invasive exotic species that out-competes native fish and organisms for food and space.

At the lower lock, we hid behind a piling as a barge worked its way around the bend to the upper lock. When instructed, we entered the lock and felt like seasoned pros when we dropped another 25 feet to where we entered the beginning of the gorge, a canyon created thousands of years ago by the falls and the rapids that tumbled nearly all the way from present-day Minneapolis to St. Paul.

It wasn't long before we approached the University of Minnesota campus and the bridge that connects the east and west banks. It was painted maroon and gold, of course, and had the University's signature "M" stamped on it in several places. Tharren is a professional photographer and had been snapping photos of every bridge on the trip but I was surprised he pointed his camera at this one because he lives in Iowa and is an avid Iowa Hawkeye fan. As we traveled beneath the bridge I gently reminded him which team placed higher at this year's NCAA wrestling championships.

Once we passed under the I-94 Bridge, the tranquility of the gorge intensified and for a few peaceful miles we saw few signs of civilization, even though we were now in the heart of a metropolitan area of nearly 4 million people. About the only unnatural things we saw were the storm water caverns, which from a distance appeared to be limestone caves. We paddled over to one and nudged our canoe up to the graffiti-filled tunnel from which water streamed into the river. Amazingly, the water looked clean, which is remarkable considering how much trash and pollution enter the storm water system.

A few miles downstream we passed through Lock and Dam #1, so named because it is the northernmost lock and dam on the river that is still in operation.

Built in 1917, it is the same size as the St. Anthony locks but has a lift of 38 feet. From there, we paddled a short distance and beached our canoe at the mouth of Minnehaha Creek. It felt good to stretch our legs as we followed the footprints of the mighty Hiawatha about a half-mile to the famous falls named in honor of his fair maiden. The falls were spectacular as the creek, still plump with near record amounts of early summer rainfall, plunged 53 feet to the pool below. There it swirled aimlessly, eventually found its direction, then rushed toward the Mississippi.

We hiked back to our canoe and continued downstream. We were barely on the river a half-hour when we reached the confluence of the Minnesota River and got out again. This is the point where soldiers, traders and settlers landed to reach Fort Snelling. We hiked a trail up the bluff to see the historic fort, treading on what is considered to be the first road in the state.

Back on the river, we paddled another four miles and glided under St. Paul's Smith Avenue High Bridge. Soon after, we arrived at the St. Paul Yacht Club, where we were graciously allowed to store our canoe for the evening free of charge. We grabbed our gear and walked along the river through Harriet Island Regional Park. We walked past the live-aboard community of the Yacht Club and continued on to Raspberry Island, where we climbed the walkway of the Wabasha Street Bridge and pushed on to our destination. We made our final ascent to an elevation of nearly 1,000 feet and made "camp." We were on the 14th floor of the Crown

Plaza hotel, on the southwest side of the building. I pulled back the heavy drapes that darkened the room and was greeted to a stunning view of the river.

Day Three

It's 9 a.m. and we're back on the river, fueled by a large breakfast we found after snaking our way through the skyway maze in downtown St. Paul. In just minutes we paddle past Raspberry Island and a small fleet of rowers floating near the dock of the Minnesota Boat Club, which was established in 1870 and claims to be the oldest athletic institution in the state. As I viewed the rowers from atop the Wabasha Street Bridge while walking to our canoe I noticed their vessels looked long and sleek, resembling brightly colored toothpicks floating in a bowl of murky water. Now, close-up, I marvel at the diminutive width of the sculls, which appear to be just wide enough to accommodate the lean bodies of the rowers. We nod at them as they get ready to dig their long oars into the river and swiftly propel themselves in the opposite direction we are traveling.

We paddle under the Robert Street Bridge and are soon beneath the Lafayette Bridge, now under construction. We pause to examine a v-shaped pier that will support the new bridge. The limestone bluff in front of us looks like a layered cake with fluffy dark green frosting. Atop that bluff is Indian Mounds Park, which this April was listed on the National Register of Historic Places because it has the strongest presence of the Hopewell Native American culture in Minnesota —

six large burial mounds believed to be 1,500-2,000 years old.

The bend in the river from St. Paul to South St. Paul resembles a parking lot. The banks are filled with massive barges that are weathered gray and pocked with rust. As we travel past the dike surrounding Holman Field airport we see the Joseph Patrick Eckstein tow boat of the Marquette Transportation Company nudging yet another barge into place. Hundreds of gulls are perched on neighboring barges and take to wing when a pleasure boater speeds by, the birds' bright white breasts shimmering in the sunlight as they soar around us. A train rambles down a track along the riverfront, further revealing that the Mississippi River is an important and busy transportation corridor.

A few miles later we glide beneath the I-494 Wakota Bridge and come to the former Rock Island Swing Bridge in Inver Grove Heights. We beach the canoe and get out so we can explore this historic structure, now used as a pedestrian pier overlooking the river. Nearby is the River Heights Marina. We are hungry so we paddle over and walk up to the Mississippi Pub restaurant, hoping to purchase a candy bar and sports drink. They had neither but instead served us a delicious burger with homemade chips.

From this point, the landscape changes again. The area along Upper Grey Cloud Island is arguably the most scenic stretch we've seen. Rounding the bend near Lower Grey Cloud Island we begin to see more pleasure boaters, slow cruising or moored at island beaches. One family in a powerful pontoon boat is making short bursts toward us, trying to teach their young daughter to water ski. After many unsuccessful attempts she finally gets her skis beneath her and glides along the river for several hundred yards. Suddenly, she loses her balance and tumbles into a blurred ball of flesh and fiberglass. She emerges from the river with a broad smile and a shout of victory.

The river widens as it passes Spring Lake in Nininger Township, which permanently became part of the river once the lock and dams were created and flooded the lake's adjoining bank. We have seven miles to go to our destination of Lock and Dam #2 in Hastings so we settle into a metered rhythm for our final push. A barge is in the main channel so we paddle closer to the shore, which requires more effort since we are out of the current.

About one mile above the dam we see an odd contraption buzzing slowly along. The makeshift raft looks like a simple tree fort built on an 8-by-8-foot wooden platform. On it are four young men, all standing and gripping the sidewall. The raft is being towed by their friend in a small fishing boat. He is sitting beneath the shade of an umbrella and has his hand on the throttle, which is wide-open yet not producing much power. With 24 miles behind us, the sight of it gives us the final burst of energy we need to reach the lock. We stroked hard to beat them to it and were victorious. Once inside the lock, a worker held out a long pole with a rope dangling from it and summoned us to it. He resembled a deep-sea fisherman and we a hungry tuna. Tharren grabbed the rope and we chatted with him as the raft pulled in behind us and the lock doors closed. In the course of our conversation the worker motioned behind us to the rafters and said, "I don't know *what* that is."

We just smiled and shrugged our shoulders. We said nothing but we knew what it was; it was four friends in the midst of living a tale that they will forever retell.

Hastings was the last stop for Tharren. He had to return to his life and responsibilities of running a business. I returned to the Hastings boat ramp with my kayak the following day to complete the final few miles of the journey. The river there is popular with pleasure boaters who like to cruise between Hastings and Prescott, Wis., just two miles away. From there they can continue downstream or head north up the scenic St. Croix River. As I paddled along, few of the power boaters paid much attention to me and I had to often paddle into their wake to keep from overturning. I quickly made it to Prescott and then traveled another two miles along the high bluffs to mile 809 and the mouth of a stream that leads to the Vermillion River. This is the end of the line on the Great River. The final two miles of the Mississippi National River and Recreation Area extend down the stream and along the Vermillion River. I returned the following weekend to explore that area.

While on the Vermillion, I saw a large brown head

swimming toward me. It appeared to be a chocolate lab until I got closer and saw the animal dive. The sharp slap of its tail told me I had seen my first beaver of the trip. I thought of the beaver and the role it played in opening this territory to European immigration, and the resulting implications for the Native Americans living here. I recalled discussing "Bury My Heart at Wounded Knee" with Tharren the first day on the river and examining sites along our route that are found in those pages. Floating in the floodplain it's easy to imagine what this land was like in the days of the Dakota. I gazed into the forest and could envision the haze from a campfire roasting wild game and hungry shadows moving toward it, eager for a feast and conversation.

The Indians have moved now, save for the few hundred Mdewakanton—those born of the water—that live on the nearby 535-acre Prairie Island Reservation. Only about 300 of those acres can support housing and the Indians are no longer able to live off the land. However, for the past 20 years they have been raising a buffalo herd to provide nutritional meat for their community. More than 100 bison now roam 187 acres of prairie land along the Mississippi River. To further support the tribe, the Mdewakanton have turned to what they call the new buffalo: gaming. The community owns and operates Treasure Island Resort and Casino, located on the reservation.

From an eagle's vantage point, the Vermillion looks like a child tagging alongside his strong father.

It runs parallel to the Mississippi through the forested floodplain. It's a quiet and scenic area that stamps a punctuation point at the end of the river's story in this area. The solitude of the tranquil backwaters gave me time to reflect upon our trip, which provided an experience unlike any other we've shared. We saw a river that for centuries has supported diverse populations of people and wildlife, and experienced a glimpse of what early settlers felt when they traveled all day by water and came upon the bustling waterfront district of Minneapolis or St. Paul. We saw a river that continues to attract people to it for a number of recreational uses, and a river that travels through backyards. We traveled at a pace of four miles an hour, which allowed us to fully absorb our surroundings. We drifted past industrial sites and considered how progress impacts the river, floated by historic sites that transported us back in time, and sat silent as we watched a spectacled monarch butterfly flutter its way across the river. We smelled the river's sweet fragrance and its toxic stench. We felt its force below us, against us, and its cool water drip on our hands from our paddles. We looked upriver and saw where it came from and peered around every bend, wondering what lay ahead. It was a classic trip. It was urban. It was wild and scenic. It was an adventure.

Explore the River

Mississippi National River and Recreation Area
Information and activities about the river corridor in the Twin Cities, including the Mississippi River Companion, a resource to trails, boat ramps and recreational opportunities in the Mississippi National River and Recreation Area
www.nps.gov/miss/index.htm

Mississippi River Boating Guides
by the Minnesota Department of Natural Resources
www.dnr.state.mn.us/safety/boatwater/guides.html

St. Paul Yacht Club
Transient and seasonal slips
www.stpaulyachtclub.org

Minnesota Boat Club
Rowing and sculling on the Mississippi River
www.boatclub.org

Padleford Riverboats
Public and private riverboat cruises
www.riverrides.com

Mississippi River Field Guide
Facts and folklore for sites along the Mississippi River in the Twin Cities by Friends of the Mississippi River
www.fieldguide.fmr.org

Minnesota's Great River Road
Minnesota's portion of the national scenic byway
www.mnmississippiriver.com

Great River Road Wine Trail
Wineries along the Great River Road in Minnesota
www.greatriverroadwinetrail.org

Mississippi River Fund
Resources to help people protect, preserve
and enjoy the Mississippi River
www.missriverfund.org

Friends of the Mississippi River
Projects to protect the Mississippi River
in the Twin Cities area
www.fmr.org

Acknowledgments

Thanks to my wife Jil Spitzack for her constant love, support and encouragement; my father Maynard Spitzack for proofreading; Leslie Martin for her keen editing skills; and Tharren Keith for his friendship and assistance with the cover design. I also thank John O. Anfinson, superintendent of the Mississippi National River and Recreation Area, for reading my manuscript and giving it his enthusiastic personal stamp of approval. The phrase "the color green" was inspired by the Rich Mullins song "The Color Green," from the album "A Liturgy, A Legacy and A Ragamuffin Band." It's a classic album about sojourning through this world. Mostly, I give thanks to God for His love, faithfulness and the beauty of creation.

Seek and you will find...
Matthew 7:7

About the Author

TIM SPITZACK is editor and publisher of a newspaper publishing company in St. Paul, Minnesota. He is also the author of *The Messenger*, published by Oaktara.

www.oaktara.com

www.timspitzack.com

Also by Tim Spitzack

The Messenger

*Once in a lifetime a story will change
your heart and your perspective...*

John Jenkins, a young journalist, is marking off time
at the small-town Marquette Messenger until he can
get into the big-league newspapers. After all, nothing
significant ever happens in a farming community, he
thinks.

Then one day Jenkins is given a routine, dull
assignment—to write the obituary of an elderly local
farmer, Alfred Gutzman. The remarkable untold
story Jenkins uncovers through his investigation,
happenstance encounters with people who knew
Gutzman, and covert visits to his farm, challenge
everything the young reporter holds dear...

*A poignant glimpse of the heart wounds of
WWII vets on both sides of the line*

CPSIA information can be obtained
at www.ICGtesting.com
Printed in the USA
FFOW04n1105220116
20693FF